Praise for *Get Real, Get Gone*

"Don't even think of buying a boat until you have read this book".

-**Tom Cunliffe**, legendary sailor and author of *The Complete Ocean Skipper*

"Rick serves up hard-headed, unsentimental, and occasionally hilarious advice... More than a how-to manual for the would-be world traveler, *Get Real, Get Gone* also tells how to live life to the fullest, and make every day an adventure...You'll learn a lot, and laugh a lot, reading this book".

-**Marjorie Preston** *Good Old Boat* Magazine

"This book is simply head and shoulders above any other source I have read. Honest, clear and utterly essential for anyone contemplating life aboard a boat as a life style. Its funny, witty and so well written you become lost instantly. The technical information is clear and very well thought out. I began to realise my first thoughts on boats and buying them were completely wrong! This book will save your life. And your bank balance. Finally it's actually written by people who live this life. I can't think of more apposite guides. Brilliant".

-**Phil Ryan** Author, composer and co-founder of *The Big Issue*

Get Real, Get Gone

How to Become a Modern Sea Gypsy and Sail Away Forever

By Rick Page and Jasna Tuta

ISBN-13: 978-1516846634

ISBN-10: 151684663X

Licence Notes

Disclaimer

For Paul and Simone

Fair winds and calm seas.

Table Of Contents

Part One
Getting Real

Introduction

For the sake of comfort, we give up knowing the world.

ANON

There is a lot to be said about being rich and living a life of luxury, or so we are continually told by television and glossy magazines. The media enthusiastically reports upon the successes and excesses of the rich and famous with a mixture of amazement and implicit adulation. The second homes built by incompetent bankers with their obscenely large bonuses or the fifty million dollars Johnny Depp gets paid to reprise his role (again!) as a slightly effeminate pirate, are all held up for our amazement and education as to what constitutes the 'good life'. The press coo over the mega-yachts of the rich and the elective surgery of the famous until it almost goes without saying that a life of pampered luxury is to be desired above all else.

What you don't hear so much about is the fantastic lightness of being and genuine advantages that can come from being less well off.

This book is a practical guide to living and exploring on a sailboat, but in many ways it is also about the spiritual benefits that come from living on next to nothing and the attitude of mind that one needs to develop in order to access them. In many ways, your success as a watery wanderer will largely depend on your attitude. If you would genuinely prefer to go to sea in a million dollar yacht full of gin and bikinis, then put this book down and get off your tushy and go and make 20 million dollars. There is nothing for you here.

But if getting real about your life and embarking upon a great adventure, on what you can realistically scrape together sets your tummy tingling, then you are most definitely in the right place.

Jasna and I do not sail past a million-dollar yacht and secretly wish it was us. No way! We know exactly what comes with that kind of vessel – the worry, the endless maintenance, the astronomical bills, the sky-high insurance, the environmental guilt and the constant vigilance of being ripped off. You can't sneak into a small anchorage or a quiet little harbour. Nor can you drop the anchor in a bay that is a little shallow or explore narrow channels or rivers. You cannot personalize your floating home or make small repairs with re-cycled materials (I have just made an instrument cover from some old bits of teak and aluminium which gave me great pleasure, cost nothing and is totally unique). No way. Once you have a million dollar baby, you have to keep her looking like she just left the shop. The rich have to protect their investment, while us sea gypsies are simply living in our homes.

We have been aboard many posh yachts and always make the appropriate noises ("ooh that is a great freezer, ahh that is a cool washing machine") but have always been happy to get back to *Calypso* - our simple little home. Why? Because we know in reality what all those flash gadgets and leather sofas cost the owner in time, worry and money. We have seen his fuel bill, we have listened to his worries about finding honest crew or a boatyard big enough to haul his huge bottom out of the water. Expensive, complicated vessels can isolate you from the very world you are hoping to discover and actually prevent you from enjoying life at sea and absorbing the spiritual gifts that are so often the bedfellows of a simpler life.

The rich throw money at problems. Us sea gypsies sort them out ourselves and with that, we become better sea gypsies. Rich sailors buy what they want. Sea gypsies buy what is essential and with that become better citizens of the Earth. Rich people tend to hide in air-conditioned marinas. Sea gypsies sit under palm trees and meet local people and gain insight. Rich people create waste by throwing away perfectly usable items under the banner of 'upgrading'. Sea gypsies fix stuff. Rich people are targets for poorer people. Sea gypsies *are* poorer people and sleep with the door open.

Hence the title of the book, *Get Real and Get Gone*. You can live in a dream world of million-dollar yachts and plastic people hopelessly marooned in the showing-off stage of their development, or with a slight change in attitude, you can 'get real' with the money you actually have (or can realistically acquire), and get gone on the greatest adventure of your life…

Chapter 1

Getting Started

In the next chapter we will show you how to start your new life as a sea gypsy as quickly as possible. You will need some money (not as much as you think, but some) and a big dollop of determination. But every day, perfectly ordinary people like you and I are 'ditching the dirt' for a better life at sea and there is no reason why you can't too. The important thing is to get started. If you already know how to sail and have a bit of money put by, you can read the last paragraph of this chapter and move on. However, if like us, you are starting out with little experience and less money, then read on...

When I (Rick) decided I wanted to ditch the dirt and become a sea gypsy, my circumstances meant I had to carry on working for another three years before I could get going, but every day I moved my plan along a little by acquiring the skills and knowledge necessary for a safe and enjoyable life at sea. Once your have a picture of your future life in your mind and truly believe it to be attainable, you will find all the motivation you need. This book aims to give you that picture by demonstrating how attainable this life is for anyone who wants it. But for now, let us look at what you can do the moment you finish this book.

Getting the Skills

Sailing is pretty easy. It is not rocket science or even French cuisine. Anyone can do it. It is not gender specific, does not require advanced motor skills or particularly high levels of physical fitness. If you can jog for a hundred meters, you will do.

You can save an awful lot of money (which can ultimately be spent on your boat) and have huge amounts of fun by buying yourself a small sailing dinghy (preferably with a mainsail and a jib, but anything will do) that will fit on top of a car. Spend a little time reading any beginners' sailing book from the library or visit any website on 'how to sail', buy a couple of life jackets, grab a friend, drive to your local lake on a day with good conditions and go and get into trouble.

With a good book and a small sailboat, you can learn just about everything there is to know about the physics of sailing and you can sell them both when you are done. You do not need to pay a fancy school thousands of dollars to learn to set an anchor, trim a jib or reef a sail. (Things actually get easier when they get bigger – it is virtually impossible to capsize a good sea boat and the boom is usually above head height when you are in the cockpit, so there is much less likelihood of it cracking you on the noggin).

Cruising courses are all very good, but most of this information is available online and can be learnt more cheaply. Courses in larger boats can be a good way to practice docking and handling a boat in close quarters, but as you will see later in this book, you are going to buy a proper sea boat (not the type of production boat that the schools buy) so your boat will handle totally differently in close quarters anyway. Do not get me wrong, I am not opposed to sailing schools (I am now a RYA qualified skipper myself). They can provide some good information and hands-on experience. However, there is no substitute for the real experience of miles under the keel as the person making the decisions, and that is what you will get in your own car-topper sailboat, sneaking up rivers and lakes. You will save a fortune and it will be fun too.

Another option is to join your local sailing club. A lot of people are put off joining a sailing club because of the Hollywood image of the snobby retired Admiral in a blue blazer and white slacks huffing and puffing over a gin and tonic and speaking in ridiculous terms nobody understands.

"By the lee!"
"Belay the helm!" and rubbish like that.

Well I am sure you can find one or two like that if you really try, but if there was ever an organization that did not deserve its stereotype, it is the local sailing club. We have visited many and have never seen a captain's cap or a blue blazer! In reality, sailing clubs are nothing like the *Carry on Sailing* image that seems so firmly lodged in most people's minds. Far from it. Most clubs are very down to earth and run by really nice people committed to the art of moving through water under sail. Sure, there are a few idiots here and there, but far less than in say, the local supermarket, but that should not stop you joining the local sailing club any more than it should stop you popping down to Asda for a carton of milk. Nor do you need to live by the sea. I first sat in a sailboat on a lake in North London.

Perhaps the best thing about sailing clubs is that (contrary to popular belief) nearly all boat owners are looking for crew and you do not have to be experienced to join in. If you know your right from left and are prepared to show up when you say will show up (even in the rain), then you will be a very popular person indeed and you can learn as you go along. Most skippers are more than happy to share their knowledge with a keen crew member. Sailing clubs also run extremely cheap sailing courses for members. I learnt pretty much everything a sea gypsy needs to know about sail trim in a week-long J24 course (a type of small sail boat with mainsail and jib) run by the tiny (but fabulous) Cairns Cruising Yacht Squadron in Australia. In short, all experience is good and much of it can be had for free. However, the closer you get to the decision making process, the more the lessons will stick.

When the weather is bad and you can't actually sail, you can teach yourself any of the other skills you need aboard a boat – navigation, weather prediction, rope splicing, extreme rum drinking, etc. The important thing is to always be moving forward.

This might sound overly casual or at least incompatible with the values of the nanny state we currently find ourselves in, and I understand your reservations. But I am not suggesting you set off around the world half-cocked. I am not suggesting setting off around the world at all.

The secret to the sea gypsy life is quite different…

Chapter 2

Getting Gone

Have you ever read any of these books that are on the market about the accessibility of sailing? Well they all have pretty much the same theme - anyone can buy a boat and sail around the world on a budget. They are normally written by the female half of a couple and once you have read about a third of the book, it becomes apparent that the other half has either been sailing since he was an embryo, is the Olympic Dinghy Champion or is an accomplished boat builder. The whole concept of 'anyone can sail around the world on a budget' then gets transformed to 'anyone can sail around the world on a budget if they happen to be married to a really excellent sailor and/or boat builder' and one is always left feeling a wee bit cheated.

I confess that two of my favourite books on budget sailing fit this description (see the recommended reading list). That is not to say that they don't have anything to offer, far from it, I love these books and have learnt a great deal from them. But in many ways, they can also be quite dangerous as they imply that it is a great idea to go ocean bashing with relatively little experience of sailing or boat maintenance.

Two years ago, Jasna and I attended a meeting of mainly American yacht owners in Mexico who were preparing to cross the Pacific. We were appalled at the lack of basic seamanship that was displayed by many of the participants. Many had never anchored before whilst others did not know how to reef their sails. One budget couple was leaving without charts (they were using Google Earth). These relatively inexperienced sailors dismissively referred to this crossing as the 'puddle jump' - further trivializing the dangers of crossing the world's largest ocean. I am sure many of them made it across and are now writing books suggesting that any fool can do it in any old dog of a boat, and that seamanship is a lot of old phooey – look at us! We did it with an iPad!

Yes, it is perfectly acceptable (though still not advisable) for you to set off around the world with very little experience if you are married to Larry Pardey or Pete Hill, but this is exactly what you must NOT do if you are truly starting from scratch. You need to build up experience, develop confidence in yourselves and your boat, discover the systems that work and those that don't, learn to move as a team (or devise systems for single handing if you are alone), find what breaks on your boat and replace it with a beefed-up version.
Does this mean that you have to become an excellent sailor before becoming a sea gypsy? NO and NO again. There is a third way, which has the benefit of getting you straight into your real adventure quickly and safely. It also has the advantage of being HUGE amounts of fun.

Buy a boat somewhere nice, where it is cheap to live, that has lots of easy sailing and move aboard.

Read the sentence above again and again, as it THE secret to getting into this life without putting yourself in huge amounts of danger or having to marry an experienced sailor/boat builder. All over the world there are great places in the sunshine with protected sailing, secure anchorages, interesting snacks and cheap beer. Some might be in your own back yard. Choose one, buy your boat there and get to work. You can fix her up while living aboard or take a cheap room somewhere if the mess is driving you nuts. You can (as we did for a while) get taken on as a 'boat sitter' on somebody else's boat while yours looks like a tip. Much will depend on the condition of the boat you buy. When she is safe to sail (notice I did not say 'finished') you can start making little trips out to local bays in good conditions until you are comfortable with your boat. You will know when this is, I promise you. Then why not try a little further afield? Maybe an overnight passage? The wind is picking up? What about reefing down this time and carrying on instead of heading back to the secure anchorage? Weather turning crap for a week? Time to do some work on your boat at anchor, hang with the other watery wanderers you meet, drink beer, swap snacks and pick up some more knowledge.

You see? In one bold move you have not just moved a little bit towards your dream to be a sea gypsy… you have become one quite painlessly!

Excellent idea eh? We know dozens of happy sailors who have used this approach. We have done it twice ourselves and it really works out well. Everybody knows that the only way to really learn a language is to immerse oneself in it fully, and the same is true for the sea gypsy life. It is indeed a rare thing (and a very refreshing one) that the right thing to do is also the most fun and the least fattening, so get the atlas out and see what lights your candle.

The first time I did this, I chose the East Coast of Australia.

The sea is relatively flat behind the protection of the Great Barrier Reef, there are thousands of beautiful anchorages and lots of helpful sailors. The second time, we chose The Sea of Cortez in Mexico, which is protected by the Peninsula of Baja California and has spectacularly easy sailing, secure anchorages, good prices and wonderful, warm people (don't believe anything you see in the movies or anything Donald Trump says about Mexicans).

There are hundreds of places all over the world to choose from. They might be close to where you live or far away with sympathetic immigration laws. In some countries like Mexico or Malaysia, it is easy to become a resident (we did). In others such as Thailand, you have to hop across the border every now and then on a spectacularly cheap and short flight or an even cheaper bus. In some places you will have right of residency such as Bora Bora, Tahiti, Moorea, the Marquesas (all officially part of France and therefore the EU). Many places in the Caribbean and most countries in the Med offer easy access to EU and UK passport holders. Some of you, who did not get caught as teenager growing marijuana (oops), could even get into the USA, where good boats are quite cheap[1]. New Zealanders have preferential visa status in Australia, the Cook Islands and Fiji, which is good news for them. There are literally hundreds of choices all over the world in warm, sunny and wonderful places. All will have different rules (which seem to change on a monthly basis), so you will need to check them out, but there is certainly no shortage of

---

[1] I have assumed a UK or Euro passport. US citizens have privileges in Canada, Hawaii, Samoa, Guam, Mexico and a variety of places all over the world. Most passport holders have preferential status *somewhere* nice and sunny

choice.

The important thing though is to pick somewhere you fancy that has good, fairly easy sailing and a number of good, cheap boats for sale. Take your little nest egg and off you go...

NO WAIT! Phew! I nearly sent you off without the most important thing of all...

Chapter 3

Getting Real

You cannot cover the world with leather, so it might be a good idea to acquire some shoes.

Buddhist Proverb

If you don't like sailing, or living on the sea, that is okay, it would be very crowded out here if everybody wanted to live on the big blue or drift around tropical paradise. There are a million other ways to be happy – pick one and good luck. If you find one that is really working for you, write a book like this, so others who feel the same way can try it too.

Increasingly though, we are meeting people who like the idea of sailing, but not the reality. With one foot in each camp and both hands on their cheque book, they set about trying to create 'Sailing Light' – a kind of synthetic, microwaveable, TV dinner version of sailing, by buying and fitting out a boat to be as much like their home on land as possible. Open almost any 'sailing' magazine and you will be overwhelmed with the marketing of products designed to make your boat more like a house - and virtually all of it is a result of modern man's apparently endless need to consume, rather than the demands of seamanship. If you want to live in a houseboat, no problem! Have at it, and good luck. Nothing wrong with that at all. What concerns me though, is that potential sea gypsies who are tempted by the romance of the sea are often drawn to sailing magazines or the local marina to help visualize an alternative future for themselves. And what do they see?

Boats that cost hundreds of thousands of dollars, full of ridiculous gadgets designed with 'sale' and not 'sail' in mind. If you are a natural consumer, happily vacuuming up all you can and judging your success or failure by how much more stuff you consumed this year compared to last (some economists call this 'growth' and genuinely consider it desirable), then what you will see in the marina will confirm your depressingly common world view. However, this can be quite discouraging for those whose motivation for jumping on the bus to the marina or picking up a sailing magazine is that they suspect there may be a better and more affordable way of going to sea.

The Good News

I am pleased to say that there is a much better alternative to simply bringing consumerism offshore. If you can block your ears to marketing, misinformation and snobbery, take a good, honest look at what resources you have, (or what you are likely to have) and make a plan that includes an affordable, small sea boat, then literally, the whole world is out there for you to discover. With the right attitude, you will be surprised how much fun you can have on the sea on a small budget. I imagine most people reading this book to be already a little excited at the prospect of becoming a small, sustainable speck on a beautiful blue ocean, having some adventures and making some new friends. If, however you remain unconvinced and secretly believe that 'getting real and getting gone' is a metaphor for 'losers on small boats' then brother, we have a lot of getting real to do if you don't want to waste the price of this book!

All we ask is that you hear us out. If at the end of this book, you are still convinced that going to sea in anything less than a mega-yacht is some kind of 'loss', then thanks for reading anyway. You are free to continue dreaming of million dollar yachts on the internet and Lara Croft in a thong. No harm done.

Though what we hope you will discover in these pages is that, with a slight change in approach, living on the blue ocean without a worry is an attainable dream and one of the last great adventures still available to ordinary people without huge resources. But there is a catch. The sea and what it asks of you, requires a different sort of human being. Twenty first century post-modern cynicism won't work here. Neither will witty put-downs serve you any advantage. Most of the values we learnt 'getting ahead' will not only prove largely useless, but can in many ways cause problems when exported to sea (see chapter 8).

The sea is the same as it has always been and you will have to develop the right attitude if you wish to travel safely upon it with the money you actually have, rather than what you dream of having. This process largely consists of spring cleaning all the messages we are constantly bombarded with by our society and media as to what constitutes a desirable boat or a successful life. You will also need a good bullshit detector to recognize all the non-essential toys and inappropriate designs that salesmen try to scare us into buying. Microsoft Windows might be on its 10th version, but the sea is most definitely Ocean 1.0.

There have been some great improvements in sailing gear for sure, but most of what you need hasn't really changed at all. The good news is (as you have probably guessed by now) that having huge pots of money, is the least important aspect of living on the sea, and may even detract from your enjoyment of your new life.

When I originally published the above picture on Facebook, it was to highlight the ridiculous ostentation of the boat in the background, which belongs to Carlos Slim – the world's richest man. One fill up of his mighty diesel tanks is more than twice the price of our modest little home *Calypso* in the foreground. I was completely stunned and surprised by the amount of people whose Facebook comments were along the lines of, "can you get me invited aboard?"

They didn't mean *Calypso.*

I was surprised and a little disappointed. I had hoped that the yuppie values of the eighties had disappeared with Wham and red spectacles. Yet this is the attitude of so many in this age where we still seem to value wealth, luxury and celebrity above all else - even above the planet. Carlos Slim's little boat uses 1000 litres of fuel an hour. We use 150 litres a *year*. All that exhaust lies on the surface of the sea and acidifies the water. What joy can you get from arriving at a beautiful bay knowing that it will one day be devoid of at least half the marine life (and probably 100% of the coral reef which is particularly sensitive to acid levels) because of people like you? I often wonder what the owner of a super yacht says to his guests when he drops his enormous anchor in such a pristine environment:

"Hey guys, come and see this now as, thanks to over-ambitious megalomaniacs like me, it might be your last chance. Enjoy!"

When you sail your modest little yacht into a beautiful, pristine bay, you can enjoy it knowing that you have done everything you can to ensure this natural beauty will survive – you have used the wind to get there, you have not acidified your environment. Your modest little re-cycled boat has not used up huge amounts of resources. Because your small boat is not full of childish toys that suck power, your electricity can be sourced entirely from the sun and the wind. You can kick back in the cool shade of your cockpit with a beer while your honest little boat nuzzles her anchor, and feel the quiet contentment that only comes from being a part of something – a feeling not available to the rich superyacht owner taking a week off from empire building to use his floating status symbol. As you reach for your sunglasses (and possibly another beer) it cannot help but occur to you that ...

Bigger is not Better.

We can simply no longer afford to look at people who are consuming massively disproportionate amounts of the planet's resources as 'successful' people. The world is straining under the weight of over-ambitious people. The philosophy of, 'the more you have, the bigger winner you are' surely belongs in the dustbin of naff, along with the hairy chest/gold medallion combo, 80s' boy-bands and drunk driving. Big motor yachts like these work against the sea and the wind by trying to overpower them with money in the form of massive diesel engines and thousands of dollars of fuel. A good sailboat (and skipper) works with the sea and therefore reaps the benefits of kinship with the world that no amount of money can buy. When you live in such a pristine environment as the ocean, there is a great deal of pleasure to be derived from feeling like a part of her, rather than her enemy. The rich boater, consuming all in his path (like some kind of marine Pac-Man) to feed his power-hungry leviathan will never know this feeling.

The environmental and spiritual aspects aside, it is also likely that waiting until you have enough money to sail away in a 70 foot luxury yacht is practically another way of saying 'staying at home'. If you believe in reincarnation, great! Maybe you can have better luck in the next life. But just in case, why not get real in this life with an affordable, small sea-boat and get gone now?

Bigger is not necessarily safer.

What makes a boat safe, will be discussed throughout this book, but good initial design, proper (and affordable) maintenance, and good seamanship are generally more important than flashy toys and electronic gizmos. Some features of million dollar yachts are actually quite dangerous.

You don't have to circumnavigate. In fact it is far better if you don't.

As stated in the previous chapter, the trick to becoming a sea gypsy quickly and safely is to buy your new floating home somewhere exotic, with easy local sailing and good facilities - then start learning your skills and pouring some sweat into her. Yet it is a peculiar truth that, should you mention your intention to buy a sailboat, the first question anyone will ask is:

"Are you going to sail around the world"?

You never get asked that question if you buy a Land Rover.

"I see you have an old Defender 110. Are you going to do her up and enter the Paris-Dakar Rally"?

Never happens.

A harmless question perhaps, but one that will come back to bite you in the bum. Say it is your intention to sail around the world and then you head east from the UK and arrive some years later back in Europe and sell your boat in France. Job done? No. There will always be some negative people back home who will derive embarrassingly high amounts of squirmy pleasure pointing out that you were a few miles short of 'around the world'.

What a few negative idiots say is of no importance to us right? But if you set yourself this goal, you will always feel you have to be moving on, even at inappropriate times. Being a sea gypsy means going with the seas, winds and currents, not fighting them in order to feel you have lived up to certain expectations, even your own. If your path takes you around the world, all well and good, but it should not be your aim. If it is your aim, then you are still hoping to 'achieve' something. The sea gypsy approach is more concerned with 'enjoying something' - rather than counting miles or joining up imaginary, man-made lines on the planet.

If you decide to go back to land after drifting around the oceans for a few years, you will not have any regrets and that is how it should be. If your path turns out to be longer, all well and good - you will enjoy it more due to the skills you have learnt. To live on the beautiful blue ocean is a gift to be treasured, not an achievement to be measured.

Integrate

So, you have chosen the country where you are going to buy your boat and are on your way to becoming a sea gypsy. All over the world there are sea gypsies like you and me and it is great to hang out with them. But to really embrace the gifts that your new life is holding out to you, you need to integrate with the local people. And that means having a stab at the language.(Come on now, don't just put the CDs by the bed and hope they enter your head by osmosis!). There are usually cheap classes available virtually everywhere and even where there isn't, you speak English right? There is not a place on Earth where somebody does not want to improve their English and most are more than happy to swap language skills with you. Your whole experience will change if you get a grip on the language – and not just when you have mastered it, but from the moment you start learning!

One often hears the phrase, "I am no good with languages". This is the biggest cop-out in the world. Sure, some people are more natural athletes than others, but we can ALL improve our fitness through exercise, and so it is with languages. If you don't make an attempt at the language, you will be consigned to speak only with people from your own culture. If that is what you became a sea gypsy for, then great! I am not here to tell anyone not to be happy! All are welcome aboard *Calypso* for a cold one! (Or at least a tepid one – due to our lack of refrigeration).

I suspect though, that most people are looking forward to mingling with other cultures and your experience in any country will absolutely flower if you can at least speak the lingo a little. Other than Paris, I have never been to a place in all my years of travel where the local people were not more than happy to help with the language. Learning the language also sends a message of respect to local people. It shows that you are trying.

The Mexicans tell a joke about the Gringos (a type of rich foreigner who invariably does not speak Spanish). They say that some Gringos only say two things:

1) "Do you speak English?"

2)"Then find me someone who does."

It might be just a joke, but it does underline a fairly appalling attitude amongst some yachtsmen who often treat local people as foreigners in their own country. I am sure you don't need telling how much that attitude will limit your experience of a place. Single people particularly will benefit from an attempt at the language – there is no better way to get a second date or break the ice on the first one, than by asking, "perhaps you could help me with my Samoan?" (Note: this seldom works outside Samoa).

The world is full of beautiful people. If you are young, free and single, then why not meet a few? I cannot think of a better way for a single person to spend his/her time than by learning the language and culture of a place through the direct experience of romance and/or furious bonking.

Learning the language will get you much better deals on boat gear too. If you can learn to say:

"OK, that is the Gringo price, but I am from Scotland where we only pay the local price" in Spanish, your costs will halve in Latin America and you will get a few laughs too.

Obviously, if you are only in a country for a few months, this is hardly possible, but once you have identified where you will be buying your boat and starting your sea gypsy life, then buy the

CDs and get cracking as you are going to be there a while. For French and Spanish, I cannot recommend highly enough the remarkable approach pioneered by Michel Thomas. An extraordinary man who escaped from a Nazi concentration camp (where he was personally tortured by none other than Klaus Barbie himself) and kept one step ahead of the Nazis by learning languages very quickly and switching identities often. He spent his post war years developing his method of language learning and has taught millions of people who thought they were 'no hopers' to speak Spanish, German, Polish, English, Russian and French. There is no paperwork with his method, so it is an ideal thing to do on watch or in the cockpit of your floating building site for an hour at the end of every day, gazing out over the anchorage with a rum-based fruit drink. (See our website for details).

Slow down, change direction

Later on in this book we will see how the need for speed and recognition makes many racing sailors fairly poor sea captains. But for now, I am referring to the common cultural habit of 'goal setting'. It has become so common in our culture to 'set goals' and then try to 'achieve' them, that the ridiculousness of this self-imposed charade goes almost unnoticed. If you cannot shake this rather ingrained western attitude, not only will the sea frustrate you, but so will most developing world cultures who are generally more fatalistic.

When I was in Kenya, I took an engine part to be fixed at a local workshop in Mombassa. I was told it would be ready "kesho". When I looked up 'kesho' in my Swahili dictionary I discovered it means, 'tomorrow'.

24

So, feeling rather pleased with myself, I went back the following day and was told the same thing. The next day I was also told "kesho". And the next. Finally, I erupted and shouted:

"You can't keep saying 'kesho' and not meaning it!"

Whereupon, a very smiley face patiently explained to me, "I am truly sorry sir, but white people not understand, 'kesho'. 'Kesho' does not mean 'tomorrow' – kesho mean, 'not today'".

That tickled me so much that it lead to further discussions about the language (which I was of course trying to learn) and it turns out that this guy (his name was 'Jenga', like the game with wooden blocks) was a fellow musician and we ended up playing together a bit and I became good friends with his whole family - who loved nothing better than to teach me Swahili and hear me mispronounce things.

I abandoned my 'goal' of leaving Mombassa in the quickest time possible and changed my goal to what was actually happening in my life – In effect, I made my goal, 'meet great people, learn Swahili and wait for my part to be fixed'. I was able to achieve this goal very enjoyably - not because it was easier or less desirable than my previous one, but because it was what was actually happening in my life, rather than what I hoped was happening in my life.

I am not suggesting that you lie down and allow yourself to be kicked around by the vagaries of chance – if we find ourselves in a rotten situation, then we must fight our way out of it - but as is so often true, the source of our unease is not usually the quality of any particular situation that we are in, but our fixation upon the idea that it should be otherwise, or that we should be somewhere else. (Gotta cover those miles and achieve my 'goals'!)

So when faced with two choices of fairly equal merit, take the one that is actually happening, not the one that you have fixated upon for no other reason than that is what you have fixated upon. This is a good skill to develop because the sea is totally indifferent to your wishes and whether you like it or not, she will often have very different ideas of where she would like you to go.

Change course, go there.

Do not fixate on your 'goals'. Goals are inventions of the human mind and, unlike sea conditions or other geographical realities, can be changed in an instant. Wind not blowing from where you want it to? Why not change course and go somewhere else? (I discovered the wonderful Percy Islands this way) or go back the way you came and enjoy that place for a while longer? You can't possibly know what the results of your actions will be, so stop fixating on your goals as if they were fuelled by anything more than the conceit that you know what the future holds. You don't. But if you think you do, you will push your boat and yourself into dangerous situations just to get 'there', which in reality does not hold any more promise than anywhere else.

Some of the best experiences are unplanned and this

becomes quite common once you set off on the largely unpredictable path of a watery wanderer. The trick of course is to try and be aware of it at the time rather than becoming frustrated that the experience you are having is not the same as the one you imagined you would be having when you set your goals.

I cannot list in this book the amount of great experiences I have had by adopting this attitude. Most of the great experiences of life happen when we let go.

Sure, some things still suck - into every life a little rain must fall. I don't think any attitude can totally eliminate that. But doesn't the success of any lifestyle lie in the ability to tilt the suck /fun ratio heavily in your favour? This is made a whole bunch easier if you can abandon the desire to achieve your rather arbitrary goals when wind and tide are against you. 99.9% of the time, you will enjoy your new destination as much as (if not more than) the original plan. Some places will still suck, as would be the case if you doggedly stuck to your original itinerary. But at the very least you will have arrived somewhere sucky, having had a good sail to get there with your body, nerves and boat in one piece and still on speaking terms with the rest of your crew.

Agendas and Schedules

I think you can already guess what I am going to say about those! But rather than bore you with more ersatz eastern philosophies, I want you to conduct a little experiment. Every time you read of a yachting accident in the press, look for the scheduling error - it is always there, largely overlooked and is usually the root of all subsequent problems. Quite conveniently, it can normally be found at the beginning of the article.

"The weather looked ominous, but I had to be at work on Monday, so we slipped our lines at 0800 and..." or,

"We left Hamilton Island for the mainland despite the rudder problems as Freddie had a flight to catch..." or

"We wanted to overtake the yacht ahead, so we were flying full sails in 30 knots..."

The story then goes on to list the terrible events that unfolded – often with serious injury, loss of life or boat or all three. Quite often, the cause of the accident is given as 'heavy weather' or 'rudder failure' or some other engineering or technical culprit, when the root cause of the accident should be listed as 'attitude problem'.

As I have said already, the sea is totally indifferent to your plans – she does not care that Claudia has a bikini wax appointment or Mark's karate class is graduating on Thursday and you have promised to go out for won tons. Put your agenda ahead of the sea, go up against it and see who wins. I know this goes against the macho image of, 'man alone against the mighty sea', but that is all it is - an image. Getting real is about seeing things as they really are, not how we would like them to be or how they are portrayed in the media. The best way to do that without constant disappointment is to learn to appreciate what is actually happening around us –

rather than constantly attempt to manipulate reality to fit our desires, or satisfy our own image of ourselves.[2]

We have become so accustomed to getting what we want right now, that immediate gratification often seems the norm. This is not just wishful thinking, but is also a dangerous attitude to take to sea. Sometimes you get pinned in an anchorage for two weeks due to bad weather. Enjoy it. Read a good book, make love with your partner, learn to speak Spanish. Wishing it were otherwise will do no good. Nor will convincing yourself that it will be 'alright to leave' when clearly it is not, in order to self-justify your wish to catch the Kentucky Derby on ESPN.

Take off your shoes. Wish in one and pee in the other. Do you see which one fills up first? Good! Now you have your proper sea gypsy head on, let's have a look at what kind of trouble we can get into picking the right boat.

---

[2] This is one of my favourite examples of such madness from *Surviving the Storm* by Steve and Linda Dashew. The brackets are mine.

"Although I did not think it was the perfect moment (to set sail)..... we would be leaving on my birthday which I thought might be auspicious. I believe in fate, so I saw small events as less portentous since the outcome was secure – some combination of circumstances would always conspire to produce the same result. I sail hoping our destiny is in the hands of a benevolent God or at least some protective force, guardian angels or the spirit of a lost father – which would protect us".

This hapless skipper was not planning a little coastal jaunt, but a 1000 mile passage through some of the world's most treacherous waters. Trusting in gods, the fates or portents is as close to criminally negligent as it is possible to get, but does make a good example of just how many people create unnecessary problems when they try to project their own image of themselves, or their personal hang-ups, onto an utterly indifferent ocean. Get real. Stick to the facts

Chapter 4

Getting the Right Boat

Your success or failure as a sea gypsy starts with your attitude. With the right attitude you can effortlessly and naturally avoid many of the mistakes made by new sailors. Many people when they first start thinking about boats (me included) dream of huge billowing sails, 10ft bowsprits, guest cabins, beautifully varnished wood, chef's galleys, teak decks - you know, all the things in the movie image. Thank Neptune I didn't have a pile of cash right then or (like so many others, including the lovely owners of the 60 foot yacht Jasna and I are currently delivering to Fiji) I would have fallen in love with a completely inappropriate, over-complicated boat. I would now be sitting in my underpants on a deserted beach somewhere, hiding from creditors and drinking myself into a rum-soaked haze whilst a stringy piece of drool cuts a path down my salt-stained stomach. In short, the wrong boat will screw you right from the start.

The cost and maintenance of boats differ wildly (even between boats of the same size) and your success as a sea gypsy starts with getting your head into the right shape so it will allow you to recognize the right boat when it appears on your radar. In other words, the image of your dream boat must also be the image of the right boat. They must *match* - and this is why we have spent so much time 'getting real' before we go shopping.

You do not want to be the computer geek sitting in his parents' basement dreaming about Lara Croft whilst completely oblivious to the cute girl next door. You need to get your head into the shape where the person you genuinely find irresistible *is* the girl next door whom you actually know, who is desirable, attainable, sustainable and has the distinct advantage of not being an imaginary computer-generated secret agent.

Take the example of John and Rose from England, who had done everything right – they had learnt to sail, grabbed their (very) small nest egg and flown to somewhere sunny and cheap with good sailing and were looking for a boat. It just so happened that there was a lovely little Bayfield 32 in great condition (good engine, great sails, new-ish rigging and wind vane self steering!) that was almost ready to go, but needed a little cosmetic work. The price was right and it would have been the perfect boat for a young sea gypsy couple. However, no amount of subtle (and not-so-subtle) hinting could persuade them away from their love choice – a huge wooden monster with leaking teak decks, ancient talurit (crimped) rigging and wooden spars.

Of course, despite the surveyor's claims to the contrary, the decks had to be completely replaced just three months later, which revealed worn chain plates, which revealed... and on the story goes. So instead of spending the rest of their already tiny budget exploring local beauty spots and getting used to their new boat, it all went on huge repair bills.

This would never have happened if the image of their dream boat had matched the image of the right boat. If they could have got the two images to match, they would now be exploring in a delightful little Bayfield 32 and becoming more attached to her by the minute. So, we most definitely need to get your head in shape before you start shopping.
(Note: The little Bayfield 32 was bought by a wily, young Norwegian couple who set sail on her after a brief stay in the boatyard. We have just left them in the paradisiacal coral atoll of Fakarava, French Polynesia, while John and Rose have returned to the UK to go back to work).

Making the right choice

There is a lot to be said for arranged marriages. Our parents, aunts and uncles are often more capable of making an informed choice of partner for us than we are for ourselves while our brains are flooded with the endorphins that accompany lust and misty-eyed romance. Yet (at least in our culture) we often ignore their advice, make our endorphin-addled choices ourselves and have extraordinarily high divorce rates as a result.

Boats are the same. Most potential sea gypsies will not be thinking rationally when they buy their first boat. Instead they will fall in love with something inappropriate and make some big mistakes[3]. So what to do, what to do...?

Well, like arranged marriages, buying the right boat will only work if you at least fancy it a bit. When your parents present you with a potential partner who is grossly unattractive, it is never going to work. But should they show up with a candidate who is peeping seductively from behind thick eyelashes...

"Well", we think, rubbing our hands, "perhaps this arranged marriage thing might be worth a bash after all?"

Hopefully, your parents will have picked your partner for good reasons other than looks and the rest you can make work.

What I am saying of course, is that the choice of boats (or partners for that matter) is not a dichotomy between 'practical and ugly' versus 'beautiful and useless'. In fact, you will have to have some attraction to your boat, because what keeps a boat sailing is *love* (silicone and WD40 help too though).

Yes, you do have to love your boat if you are to put all the hours and everything you own into her. Without love there is no motivation to spend the extra day fixing her properly or to check the bilge pump one more time. There definitely has to be some initial attraction to begin with, but hopefully this book

---

[3] Although it would give us great pleasure, practicality and finance prevents us from personally visiting all the boats our fellow sea gypsies are thinking of buying, but do feel free to drop us a line though our website on www.sailingcalypso.com for an unbiased opinion

will steer you away from the spectacularly bad choices that potential sea gypsies are making every day and help you fall in love with the right boat. At the very least, it is worth spending some time correcting the images that yacht builders and magazines are so keen to install in our heads as desirable, and replacing them with something more wholesome.

The Ideal Boat for the Sea Gypsy Life

I disagree with anyone who says there is no such thing. In fact I think there are many such things. Think of finding the ideal boat like developing a healthy lifestyle. There are a million ways to have a healthy lifestyle – all of them different. There will be certain healthy foods that you like, that I don't. You might like to take your exercise swimming and doing yoga, while I might prefer kayaking and walking. So, I am not saying that everybody needs to follow the same path in order to have a healthy lifestyle - there are as many possible healthy lifestyles as there are people. However, what we can say with total confidence, is what is *not* conducive to *any* healthy lifestyle: Lying on the couch all day, smoking cigarettes, scoffing endless Happy Meals washed down with Bacardi Breezers is bad for everyone's health – one's preferences, opinions or personality do not enter into it. There is simply nobody on this planet who can use this regime to get healthy (no matter what the marketing people might say).

Boats are the same – I can't tell you which boat to like as everybody has different tastes. It is far safer (and less dogmatic) to concentrate on what we as sea gypsies definitely do NOT want in a boat and leave the rest up to you. Having said that, it is important to remember that not *everything* is a matter of personal preference - there are certain realities that are beyond the realms of mere opinion or personal choice. For example, it is not my 'opinion' that extreme racing keels fall off more often than traditional long keels. It is a fact - and we do not have the luxury of choosing whether it is true or not any more than we can choose to believe that smoking and scoffing endless hamburgers is the path to a healthy lifestyle. The trick is to know the areas where we can apply our personal choice and those where we are pinioned by the facts.

With this in mind, I have made three lists below and they are a good place to start. I have split the recommendations into three categories.

1. Not on My Watch
2. Not Ideal, but do-able
3. Annoyances you will have to change once you have bought the boat

The titles are pretty self-explanatory, but at the risk of labouring the point here, we would like to remind all potential watery wanderers that a yacht can (and often does) cost a fortune. If you have unlimited finances you will have to do battle with the confusion that will arise from the following advice, along with the inevitable feelings of disappointment that accompany the realization that you have picked up the wrong book. If you do not have unlimited resources, then the type of question you should be asking is not, "Wouldn't it be great to have a walk-in freezer?" but, "can we really afford to drop out and see the world on our own private yacht or is it be dream?"

The answer (I am ecstatic to say), is a resounding "yes" – if you avoid EVERYTHING on the first list, as many things as possible on the second and as many recommendations in the rest of the book as your love-addled brain will allow.

Good luck and fair winds!

Before we get to the first list, I would like to say a few words on boat design in general.

Forty years ago, boat design was dominated by great designers like Olin Stephens, EG Van de Stadt, Bob Perry, Bill Dixon, Jeremy Rogers, Laurent Giles, Francis Herreschoff, etc. They designed boats of a high standard to resist all that the sea was likely to throw at them. To these honest designers, it seemed so obvious that potential buyers would want such seaworthiness as a prerequisite – above all other considerations - that it went unquestioned for years.

Then some clever spods in marketing realized two very interesting facts about boat buyers. Firstly, that most boat buyers would never take their boat offshore. So why build a boat for an offshore yachtsman, when for far less, you can build a much lighter boat that will race around the buoys and be easier to park in the marina, thereby allowing the owner to get to the bar quicker to brag about his victory?

Secondly, if a man (and it usually is a man - Jasna and I are the exception, not the rule) wants to buy a sailboat, he has to clear that idea with his partner. What do you think impresses the wife more at the boat show, the reinforcing on the deck/hull joint or a nice guest cabin with polished marble surfaces in the en suite bathroom?

The Brits (not un-typically) were unable to respond to this market trend and continued to make good sea-boats nearly all of which (including Southerly and Moody who both collapsed recently) went bust or were taken over. On the European continent though, many boat builders embraced this design approach totally. Windows got bigger to create lighter interiors, galleys got flashier, toilets became electric and transoms got increasingly wider to impress your guests with a large aft cabin and en suite. Rudders became lighter and unsupported (easier to steer and park in marinas). Keels got thinner and deeper (more windward performance for club racing and cheaper to build and transport). Davits were added to transoms (to store dinghies that had now become too large to fit on deck) and a whole rack of un-seaworthy, yet eminently marketable ideas were incorporated into normal yacht design.

I am sorry to say that at least half (probably more) of the yachts you will see advertised fall into this category. To survive in a brutal economic climate, the boat builder must increasingly concern himself with the first user buying a new unit at the boat show with his wife (the builder doesn't make any money when you sell it on) and you cannot make your design stand out by spending your budget reinforcing the bulkheads or making a hull that will last fifty years.

There is some good news on the horizon though! These types

of boats are immensely popular and all the lemmings flock to them, leaving you (the wily sea gypsy with more neurons than dollars) to get a real sea-boat for a fraction of the price of the shiny 'plastic fantastics' that you see tied up and looking almost identically shiny in every marina in the world.

You must learn to shut your eyes to fancy gadgets, large motors, huge aft cabins, water makers, freezers, bow thrusters, ice makers, microwaves, even generators, and develop a new set of eyes for the important things such as small, strong portholes, water-tightness, proper construction, supported rudders, good sized properly attached keels, reinforced bulkheads, good deck to hull joints, strong anchor points for the rigging, etc

So what we all really need to do is stop letting marketeers decide for us what is attractive and learn to look at boats (or people, or anything for that matter) with a new set of eyes. Obviously a good surveyor will help, but he can only survey the boats you point him at. So here (finally! Sorry for banging on) are some tips as to what you should most certainly NOT be looking for or consider desirable in the real world.

Not on My Watch

Extreme Fin Keels. All Spade Rudders

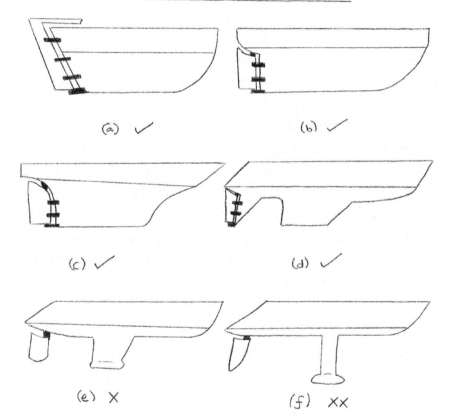

KEEL AND RUDDER ARRANGEMENTS

(a) ✓

(b) ✓

(c) ✓

(d) ✓

(e) ✗

(f) ✗✗

In the diagram on the previous page, I have sketched the most commonly found keel and rudder arrangements. I have exaggerated the diagrams to show how the rudders are attached. The first four make good boats for a sea gypsy. They have long (or long-ish) keels attached over a goodly portion of the hull or integral to it. The rudders are well attached, well protected and supported at the bottom.

The boats (e) and (f) have spade rudders and narrow fin keels. As shown, a spade rudder is unsupported, unprotected and simply hangs down from the hull on a stick. Narrow fin keels and spade rudders give you the best warning sign that the designer has made a boat for the weekend sailor, or the racing enthusiast with deep pockets. Despite what the salesman or owner may say, you are neither of these. This is not a good boat for the sea gypsy life and don't let anyone tell you otherwise. Many sailors will claim this configuration is fine, but this is due more to human psychology than engineering principle. There is also a tendency amongst sportsmen to confuse safety with success.

For example. If I decide to go over Niagara Falls in a barrel (as many have) and I survive (as slightly less have), is it now true that going over Niagara falls in a barrel is a safe or sensible thing to do? No, of course not - even when I stand in front of you – a happy, experienced barrel-jockey, as 'living proof' that it can be done without any problems. Furthermore, if it is your intention to go over Niagara falls every day, what alterations would you imagine appropriate to your mode of transport? Would you be shaving bits off it to make it faster? If you hope to get away with it regularly, I imagine some beefing up of the barrel would be the first sensible thing to do.

Frequency changes the goal posts.

Think of an activity that carries a 100 to 1 chance of killing you. Do it once and you will probably get away with it. Do it 200 times and the odds are likely that it will kill you. You have to have a different outlook when you repeat something risky. I spent sometime in my thirties learning to skydive and I was impressed how seriously the 'old hands' took their safety. They did not become more reckless with time, but more safety conscious. This is because skydiving carries a risk of about 100,000 to one. If you only ever do one skydive the odds are stacked in your favour. But many of these guys are closing in on 3000 jumps and that makes their odds of becoming a meat bomb too close to be comfortable. So they come up with better safety protocols and gear – far in excess of what many young skydivers find appropriate, to stretch the odds back on to their side. Because as they so rightly say:

"There are old skydivers and bold skydivers, but no old, bold skydivers"

You need to keep this in mind when you buy a boat for the sea gypsy life.

Yet I can already hear a number of sailors (including respected, published authors, I am embarrassed to say) huffing and puffing about how they crossed the Atlantic Ocean in their Bavaria Match (a model of boat with an unsupported spade rudder and extreme fin keel which fell off so regularly they had to be recalled by the factory) without a problem. Well whoopee-do. Good for you! It must be safe then! Get the barrel ready for Niagara!

Do not be fooled by some famous sailors' lack of engineering knowledge or statistical literacy. The fact that somebody won the lottery does not mean that person made an intelligent investment decision. Get a boat with a decent keel and a skeg-hung (supported) rudder. It might save your life. It will certainly save you money when you run aground (you will)[4]

Once you are out sailing, you will meet plenty of sailors who have narrow fin keels and spade rudders and are quite happy. Always remember that these are the ones who are left! The others got bored of the constant expense or worse. Our very good friends on the Sweden Yachts 45 *Queenie,* lost their previous Sweden Yachts 45 when their unprotected spade rudder hit some ocean debris - and they are by no means unique.

Do not become a victim of advertising. There is no way that making a keel joint smaller and leaving the rudder unprotected leads to a stronger boat. This is sales talk. Make like Odysseus and strap yourself to the mast and stick your fingers in your ears.

Some salesmen (and again I am embarrassed to admit, some famous sailing writers) like to claim that the slight increase in speed achieved by a lighter built, fin keel and spade rudder

---

[4] One famous writer of cruising manuals actually claims that fin keels are better because boats with fin keels are easier to retrieve when shipwrecked on a reef! This is the equivalent of saying that an aircraft made of pizza boxes is safer because the parts won't rip through your body when it crashes. Ridiculous, I know, but it goes to show, how thin a straw some people are prepared to grab hold of in defence of their competitive edge or larger aft cabin

boat is justifiable on the grounds that, "a fast passage equals a safe passage". They claim this because weather predictions become almost useless after about three days. The theory is that, by the judicial use of speed, your faster, lighter boat can whiz from one safe haven to another and never have to deal with ugly conditions.

You don't need to be a boat designer to see the holes in this argument. Having said that, there could be something to be said for this theory if the following conditions were also true:

- you never made any passages longer than three days

- weather forecasts of three days or less were always accurate (!)

- you never had a problem with your boat that delayed your arrival (your unprotected rudder smashed to bits by colliding at high speed with floating debris for example)

- you were never becalmed.

- diesel engines never broke down

- you always have an infinite supply of clean fuel

- you live somewhere other than the real freaking world

The last one is particularly important. Say what you like about us sea gypsies, but the real world is something we cannot ignore. To become a successful long-term voyager, you must really learn to tune out the opinions of salesmen, racing sailors, marina queens and the designers who pander to them. Instead, learn to see what will really help you at sea. Developing an aversion to extreme fin keels and unsupported spade rudders is a really good place to start getting real.

Large Boats

Very nice to look at, I know, but remember the title of this book. Is looking at 50 foot yachts, 'getting real'?
It goes without saying that the cost of boat maintenance (as well as marina fees, dockage, transit fees etc) rises with size of boat. What is not so well understood is that this is not a linear relationship, but an exponential one. When I say 'exponential' I really mean it too – no metaphors here! A 50-foot boat can easily be fifteen or twenty times more expensive to buy and maintain than a 25 foot boat – not twice as much as you might first imagine.

Even a small increase in length can have a hugely disproportionate effect on weight and therefore running costs. For example, our first boat (a steel Van de Stadt) was 34 feet (10m) and weighed 6 tons. Our current boat is around 7% longer, but weighs 30% more. All that extra weight needs to be driven forward, so bigger sails are needed, stronger rigging, thicker anchor chain, bigger engine etc, etc. A Potential sea gypsy needs to think not "what size boat can I afford" but, "how small a boat can I live on".

I cannot answer that question for you, but I can warn you that boats are getting bigger and bigger as more affluent, weekend sailors and retired professionals drive the market. But to give you our own example: our current boat is 36 feet and that is possibly even a little large for a sea gypsy couple. Unless you intend doing a bit of illegal charter (see chapter 10), 36 feet is more than a couple really need (we have some friends who are bringing up two kids on a 36ft boat!). Remember that the most famous cruising couples of all time (the Pardeys and the Hiscocks) both sailed for years on boats under 30 feet. The Pardeys' original boat was just 24 feet 9 inches.

The advantages in cost (both buying and maintenance) of a small boat are fairly obvious, but there is another major money saving advantage that is often overlooked. Good quality stuff (ropes, shackles, sails, rigging etc) for your boat often cost twice as much as cheap Chinese knock-off, but can last up to 5 or 6 times as long. With a small boat you are more likely to be able to afford the good stuff because you will need less of it, thereby cutting your long-term maintenance costs quite substantially and making your boat safer as well. Imagine your floating gypsy home is in need of new standing rigging. A large boat can easily cost $15,000 to rig, whereas your small boat might be nearer $3000. Which boat is likely to go ahead and do the work and which boat is maybe going to push it for another year? Small boats are cuter too! Our little traditional cutter often steals admiring glances from bigger fancier boats. That would be a bit annoying to witness from the cockpit of your million dollar yacht!

The important point to remember then (and one of the principle messages of this book) is this:

Getting real means buying small. You will not regret this.

Multihulls (Catamarans and Trimarans).

Multihulls have their aficionados and I include myself amongst them, but they are not a good choice for your first command. They are more expensive to buy, maintain, lift and park than monohulls. Therefore you will get a much better mono for your small nest egg in a 'seaworthiness per dollar' sense.[5]
Sure, all that space is luxurious, but the budget conscious sailor should concern herself with quality, not luxury. Imagine you were buying a used car. What kind of Ferrari would you get for $2000? A very dodgy one with a whole raft of problems. You might get a great little Honda though, so assuming that you do not have unlimited finances (which is the basic assumption of this book) then always go for the monohull.

Furthermore, multihulls are much less idiot-proof than monohull boats. If you get caught with too much sail up in a sudden squall (happens all the time), a monohull will usually heel over and spill all the wind from her sails, popping up unharmed once the gust has passed. A multihull cannot do this and will have to disperse this energy in other ways – perhaps by blowing a sail, breaking the rig (and therefore risking the mast) or flipping over. Remember that once a multihull boat is inverted, it will not naturally right itself again. A monohull usually will (unless you have left all the hatches open, in which case you really had it coming). As a new

---

[5] There are two possible exceptions to this rule. James Wharram catamarans and Jim Brown trimaran designs are both aimed at the budget boat builder. The Wharram design can be easily beached to carry out routine maintenance and has a big following amongst budget sailors. All the other drawbacks of multihulls still apply so, while Wharram catamarans and Brown trimarans are both great vessels, I do not recommend them as a good choice for your first boat.

bluewater sailor, you will be on a very steep learning curve and it is only natural that you will be making plenty of mistakes - it just depends how severely you want to be punished for them. Also, the performance into the wind of most multihulls is not as good as most monohulls, meaning that should you wish to go in that direction, you will need to burn fuel. You can forget beating off a lee shore in most multihulls.

Unless you already own or have significant experience in multihulls and fairly deep pockets, I would leave them for next time. You have enough to learn for now.

Wooden Boats

I know, I know, they are lovely looking and have been around for hundreds of years and have souls, but a wooden boat will screw you as thoroughly as a Caracas cathouse. I am aware that the Pardeys and the Hiscocks both had wooden boats, but the Hiscocks sailed in the fifties when most boats were still made from wood and Larry Pardey happens to be a gifted wooden boat builder. Also, in the fifties and sixties, there was still plenty of old growth teak and mahogany around. So forget dreams of wooden boats and empty your recycle bin of pictures of old wooden boats unless you want to be constantly working and paying for your dream rather than living it.

Teak Decks

Again, very pretty looking. The broker will point out how nice they are to stand on (except in the sun, when they are hotter than a waffle iron). However, we are looking at a used boat right? And those teak decks will need replacing at some point at enormous expense. Even if they have a bit of life left in them, most of them leak like crazy and drip on your sensitive (read, 'expensive') electronics (for this reason, the CT41 owners' club refers to itself as the 'leaky teaky' club). Most people choose not to replace them when the time comes anyway. Instead, they rip them up and fibreglass the decks. This is a much better solution, but do not underestimate how much time and money this will cost – often into the tens of thousands. There are so many boats for sale without teak decks, why punish yourself? Teak decks on steel boats are such a stupid idea that I cannot even comment on it other than to say one word. No.

Ferro Cement Boats

Don't get me wrong, there are some great ferro cement boats out there. Most of them though, are dogs.
There was a bit of a craze for cement in the 70s amongst home boat builders. The ferro cement boats were (supposedly) easy and cheap to build. Apparently the hulls were only half as expensive to build as hulls using other materials. However, as a hull only represents about 20% of the cost of building a boat, the overall savings could only have been around 10% - hardly worth it considering the re-sale value of cement boats is about the same as Enron shares.

My main objection to ferro cement boats is that they vary enormously in quality and are virtually impossible to survey accurately – meaning that you put your little nest egg at enormous risk when buying one. Don't forget that you will need to invest time and money in your boat once it is bought and eventually try and recoup some of the cost when you sell it.

All around the world, there are ferro cement boats that have been on the market for years and are now being offered at a fraction of the original asking price as they slump under their own weight, forgotten in the boatyard. You might be tempted to snap one up, but my advice is to forget it. They are heavy (remember what we said about the knock-on effect of weight?) difficult to sell, difficult to sail, virtually impossible to insure and most of them are as ugly as a burning pug that has been put out with a fireman's shovel. Furthermore, despite their bulk, they have the worst resistance to point loading (such as hitting a submerged object like a reef or shipping container) of any boat building material. Do you really want to invest your time, your soul and your money into this boat?

Very Tall Masts

Very tall masts are great for racing, but impart far too much strain on the rigging, chain plates (and ultimately, the hull) to be practical for sea gypsies. Tall masts also impart a larger 'turning moment' (the force that will capsize you). Stick to single spreader masts or double spreader at a pinch.

Experimental Rigs

Pretty much any rig will get you where you are going, some faster, some easier to handle, some better to windward and some more balanced than others. Don't sweat it too much. Just stick to the tried and tested ones and avoid experimental rigs (such as the aero rig). I will give a quick rundown of the advantages of the different rigs in chapter 5.

Large Windows

In their never-ending quest to sell boats by appealing to non-sailors (sorry for the implied sexism, but it is usually wives), many manufacturers (particularly catamaran manufacturers) are trying to make a boat seem increasingly more like an apartment. What is the first thing you look for in an apartment after location? Good light! So they introduce large windows and even double-glazed sliding patio doors. These are undesirable for two reasons. Firstly, when conditions get ugly, the large window is nowhere near as tough as a small, bronze or stainless steel porthole with toughened safety glass in the middle. Furthermore, should they fail, they are much more difficult to plug up. (I can plug my little portholes with a pillow, but I will never need to because they are small and robust). Some manufacturers even place large windows near the waterline in order to give the guest cabins good light. I dread to think what happens when a fender rolls on to them during a surge in a marina, but the sound 'pop' seems to spring far too easily to mind.

Secondly, light interiors are only considered desirable by us westerners because we have generally lived for generations in countries with crap weather. Allowing a lot of light into your boat is a truly horrible idea in the sunnier climes, where most of us intend to sail. The sun pouring through your massive windows will soon turn your boat into a blinding oven. Then of course to be comfortable, you will install air conditioning and then to run the air con, you will buy a generator, which will result in you living in the marina because it actually looks like good value compared to burning petrol all day. Wow! Could it be that this type of boat was actually designed with marina living in mind? (Now you are getting it! Keep that head on!)

Your boat must be a comfortable place to be – even in the tropics. And that means keeping the sun out and letting the breeze in. If the heat is forcing you out all the time, your budget will suffer as well as your decision making. How hard is it to wait for the right weather window while sipping an iced tea in your comfortable, cool boat? A lot easier than pacing around in an oven like a half-done prawn. When you look at a boat, keep in mind that it is not a luxury hotel room and you will not be living in the manufactured environment of a marina, but sailing in the beautiful, wondrous, unpredictable, real world.

Not Ideal, but Do-able

The items on this list are not deal-breakers, but need to be thought about. Obviously, if a boat is wonderful in every other way, having one or two things on this list should not deter you, but you should definitely factor them into your offer.

Inaccessible Water and Fuel Tanks

Ugh! Fell for that one myself. Our boat *Calypso* had a completely inaccessible fuel tank. What was worse, it was ordinary mild steel (sometimes euphemistically called 'black iron') and was rotting. To make matters worse, the whole boat had been built around this monster and to remove it involved destroying the entire galley, half the beautiful teak joinery, (which of course had been glued, not screwed together), some of the cabin sole, 3 floor joists and virtually all the wiring (which had been routed across the tank).

Have a good look at the tanks and imagine what you will do when they inevitably spring a leak. When we were looking at *Calypso*, I realized that we would have to replace the fuel tank at some point and went back to the broker and dropped my offer by 10,000 USD. The seller consulted with the surveyor and they accepted my reasoning and my offer. It took me about three weeks and US$2,000 to re-fit two cross-linked polyethylene tanks, so I suppose I am up on the deal, but it was a colossal pain in the arse. I have seen many boats with good sized, totally removable stainless or aluminium tanks. There is no reason for you to settle for a boat with badly thought out fuel or water tanks without a considerable price reduction.

Lifting Keels

I love lifting keels. I love sneaking into anchorages that have only a few feet of water or exploring up rivers and estuaries. But there is no doubt that for ocean sailors, lifting keels are a pain. They are constantly causing trouble, are less effective to windward and are expensive to replace/repair. Legendary sailor and sailing writer Jimmy Cornell noted in a survey of owner satisfaction, that owners of boats with lifting keels were the least satisfied of all boat owners. (He now owns one, so work that out!). If sneaking up rivers is your thing and you don't intend to cross oceans, then a lifting keel is probably a good idea. If you wish to do both, then a good compromise is to buy a boat with a fixed keel of moderate draft (depth). Our last boat came with a choice of deep or moderate fixed keels. Deep for racing, moderate for cruising. For those potential sea gypsies who do not consider a small reduction in windward performance too high a price to pay for sneaking up shallow rivers, choose a moderate fixed keel. We chose our first boat because it had the shallower keel and never regretted it.

In-mast furling

Complicated, expensive, prone to failure at the worst possible moment. Avoid unless the boat is such a bargain that you can afford to retrofit a normal mainsail. Unfortunately, most sellers consider in-mast furling a positive attribute and will set their price accordingly.

Electric Winches, Electric Furlers.

All electric gadgets break down. The more electric gadgets you have, the more breakdowns you will have. The more

---

breakdowns you have the more bills you will have and the more bills you have the more you will need to work and the less time you will spend living your new gypsy life. Furthermore, electric furlers and winches eat electricity at an alarming rate which means more solar panels, larger batteries, possibly a generator, all of which make your boat heavier, requiring more fuel under engine, more strain on the rigging, more maintenance, more money etc., etc. The knock-on effects are certainly worth considering. However, the biggest problem with electric furlers is when they go wrong and you are stuck with all your sail up in a 50 knot squall and feeling like a total dufus. I know that the manufacturers are keen to point out that there is a manual handle should the motor fail, and I could probably work with that. But this is only because I have the requisite muscles and skills built up from grinding winches manually for years. It is also worth remembering that you will need to crawl up the pitching deck in darkness (for some reason these things always fail at night) and work out where to stick the emergency handle, if indeed you have been able to locate it. We found ourselves in an interesting variation of this predicament when delivering a Garcia 60 to Fiji recently. We located the manual handle, removed the inspection plate only to find that the mechanism had shifted within the housing, preventing us from inserting it (see pic opposite).

You get the point? Complicated devices in boats will fail in ways that surprise even the designers themselves. On the other hand, a simple manual furler is virtually indestructible, easy to operate and super-reliable. Furthermore, if there is a problem, you will feel it. An electric furler will not notice and keep applying force, which may cause a much greater problem.

Don't forget that we are on a budget here! The seller of the boat with all these fancy toys on board will certainly want to collect some beer tokens from you in return for all his flashy electric gadgets. Far better to walk away and spend your gypsy chips on the simple, more important things. You can still make an offer on this type of boat, just knock off the money it will cost to replace all this stuff with simple, manual solutions – though I don't think the seller will be too happy, as some of these electric furlers are up around the $15,000 mark!

Annoyances you will need to change on your boat once you have bought it

Even if you have taken your time, found the right boat, negotiated well and are now the proud owner of a proper sea boat with a good keel, hull, skeg-hung rudder, rig and sails, it is still quite likely that you will have to change a few things. Even well made sea boats need to appeal to non-sailors, plus the former owner(s) may have made a lot of misguided alterations.

When we bought *Calypso*, the previous owner had removed the self–steering and added a shade bimini that was so high, it was impossible to trim the mainsail correctly. We have re-instated the self-steering and lowered the bimini accordingly. There are as many types of minor annoyances as there are boats, but here are some of the more common ones I have observed.

Electric only water taps

Either replace them with manual foot pumps and sell the electric pump on ebay (recommended) or put a manual foot pump in tandem. You must be able to access your fresh water easily in the case of complete electrical failure. Furthermore, if your precious fresh water is un-pressurized, nobody can leave the tap on.

Many galleys (kitchens) and heads (toilets) do not have a salt water supply. Change this. If the only available water is salt, then people will use it. On *Calypso* we have an electric pump to the salt water supply only, and this is what we use most of the time for washing up, hand washing, etc. We have also added a little extension at the salt water intake, which allows us to turn this pump into an extra bilge pump at the flick of a valve (you never know!)

Electric heads (toilets)

Electric heads use a large amount of electricity if used correctly. Have a couple of guests on board for a few days, feed them a good curry and they can flatten your batteries on their own without any help at all. Once you become aware of how much electricity they suck from your batteries, you start letting the button go as soon as the bowl is clear, rather than holding the button on for a good twenty seconds to clear the pipes as you should. This inevitably leads to calcifying of the pipes and blockages which will need to be removed by opening the pipes which are often under a good deal of pressure. This is not a fun job. On *Marutji* we used to call this job "Pippy Longstocking". (See if you can guess why).

With a good manual head, you can pump gallons of seawater through the whole system at no cost to your batteries and keep your pipes clean for longer. Manual marine heads are one of the few surprisingly cheap items you will need for your boat, so go and get one. Buy the service kit while you are there and you will have many years of stress-free poo. We have a Jabsco which is by no means the high end of the market, but has worked fine for 10 years.

Not enough reef points on the sails.

Many sailboats have only two reef points in the mainsail. You will need at least three. Four is great for heaving-to in the ultimate storm, but three is generally considered enough.

Expensive dinghies with powerful outboards

See chapter 16, but generally speaking, get rid of them and get something more durable and less attractive to thieves.

Davits

These are the things you often see on the transom of yachts with a dinghy hanging off them. Take them off and sell them. They are a terrible idea on a blue-water boat. Assuming you have sold your turtle-liquidizing rib with its enormous motor, you won't need them anyway. A boat on davits is a liability in bad weather – a big wave will eventually deposit itself right in your dinghy and either destroy the dinghy, the davits themselves, or rip the davits right out of the transom leaving a gaping hole. Also, if your dinghy is hanging off the back of your boat, where are you going to put your wind vane self-steering? (more on that in chapter 13).

Furthermore, as davits are the 'stair-lift of the sea', getting rid of them will have the added benefit of not making you look like a geriatric old codger.

Gensets

A small boat with a genset is simply not set up properly for life at sea. This boat either has too many electrical appliances or not enough solar panels (probably a mixture of both). A well set-up sea gypsy boat does not need a genset – they are noisy, expensive to run and maintain, heavy and environmentally undesirable. In a crowded anchorage they annoy the crap out of everyone and make the owners extremely unpopular. They also rely on having enough fuel around to use them. Sell it and set your boat up with solar power as described in chapter 14 – you may even make a small profit which you can put towards a wind turbine.

Tiny Cockpit Drains

Nearly all boats have undersized cockpit drains. This means that should a big wave enter your cockpit, it will not drain quickly and this will compromise your boat's ability to rise to the next wave. It will be to your advantage if you can improve matters before heading offshore. At the very least, remove the perforated grills that guard their intakes and make sure that the hoses and outlets are super clear.

No Good Sea Berths

At the time of writing this chapter, Jasna and I are delivering a posh 60ft, two million dollar yacht to Fiji. The saloon has great curved sofas and fancy king sized beds in the forward and aft ends of the boat, but not one good sea berth in the middle. A good sea berth must be in the centre of the boat where the pitching is less and have a lee cloth or lee board to stop you flying across the saloon each time you roll.

You will need as many of these as there are people off watch. In most cases, that means one, but two is nice for when you have guests or you are both below, hove-to in bad weather (more on that later). You may not have to make huge structural adjustments (a mattress on the floor with a lee cloth might work) but you will need somewhere appropriate to sleep in a seaway.

Handholds

Most boat seem to be lacking in handholds (you would think two million dollars would buy you some good hand-holds, but apparently not). When you are next out in a stiff breeze, pay attention to what you are grabbing hold of and make a list of where it might be prudent to add more handholds.

Inadequate Fuel filters

Many marine diesel engines are simply marinised vehicle or agricultural engines and are often fitted with the same fuel filtering capabilities they employed on land. Marine engines have higher filtering demands due to the variability of fuel quality in different countries and the increased risk of ingress by salt water. Check your diesel engine. If it has one fuel filter only (normally attached to the engine itself) then you need to upgrade. There is a company called Racor who specialize in filtering. Google them and give them a call. You will need at least two more filters with water traps to ensure your precious diesel engine is protected.

Badly Aligned Engines

A badly aligned engine will destroy the cutless bearing (where the drive shaft leaves the boat), create vibration, create leaks in the stuffing box (or stress a drip-less seal) and stress the coupling and transmission. So it is quite important to make sure the old fiery stinkbox is properly aligned.

I have done quite lot of work on diesel engines and pretty much all of them are badly aligned. Alignment seems to be the most commonly ignored step in the power train. An hour or two spent sorting this out will pay dividends. I have occasionally seen engines that do not have any adjustment in the engine mountings and therefore cannot be aligned in any case. If the boat you are buying is set up like this, then include the cost of some stock shim material (thin metal sheets of predetermined thickness) or better still, some new, adjustable engine mounts in your calculations.

There are many other possible annoyances, but these are the ones I find most often on the greatest number of boats. I would love to hear from anyone who feels I have left out something important or who has found a very odd 'improvement' on their boat. Drop me an email if you get a moment when you are not upside down in the bilge.

Chapter 5

Getting the Right Rig

A lot has been written on this subject and everyone has his favourite rig. The Hiscocks had a Bermudan sloop, Annie Hill and Blondie Hasler had junk rigs. Bernard Moitessier and Robin Knox Johnston preferred the ketch rig. The cutter rig is becoming increasingly popular amongst long-term voyagers. All of them have something to recommend them and all of them will get you there.

The subject is an exhaustive one and I suggest not getting too hung up on it. Here however, is a quick run-down of the rigs you will most commonly find on yachts for sale.

The Bermudan or "Marconi" Sloop

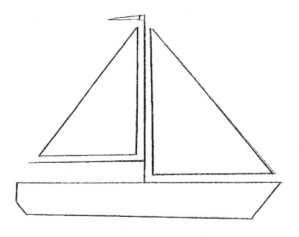

This is undoubtedly the most popular rig, but not necessarily the best for sea gypsies. The Bermudan rig owes its popularity not so much for its suitability for long term voyaging, but because it offers the fastest performance to windward for racing sailors - and racing design influences all yacht design.

Plenty of people sail this type of rig quite happily. However, downwind, they are very average indeed – often needing specialist sails and poling arrangements that are complicated and often difficult to operate in heavy sea conditions. Avoid very tall masts as the stresses are too much for a long-term voyager.

The Bermudan Cutter

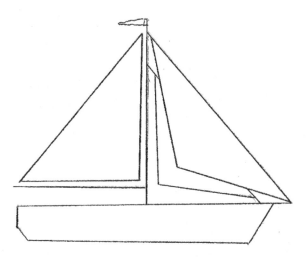

Similar to the sloop, the cutter differs by 'cutting' the foresail into two. This allows the operator to drag the centre of effort (the point on the boat that is the combination of all the wind loads) in towards the middle of the boat, which reduces stresses in heavy weather.

Two foresails are not as efficient to windward as a single, larger foresail, but this is easily overcome by using a larger foresail (without the staysail) for windward work. *Calypso* is a cutter and we find her a good, versatile rig. She suffers from all the same problems downwind as the Bermudan sloop

The Bermudan Ketch

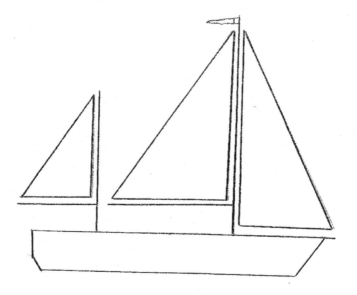

I have often heard it said that historically, the only purpose of having two masts was to make the sails smaller and therefore easier to handle and that since sail handling techniques have

improved, the ketch rig is now obsolete. To hold this view is to overlook some other advantages of the ketch rig. By spreading the sail area fore and aft (rather than up) they need less weight in the keel for balance than the taller-masted sloop and this means shallower draft and generally less strain. Furthermore, spreading the driving force over two masts means that the point loads on the rigging, turnbuckles, swages, chain plates and ultimately the hull, are all reduced. A ketch rig can also be very finely balanced and therefore easier to steer. They also heave-to beautifully (see chapter 8). Also it is helpful to remember that hardly anybody these days designs a ketch as a competitive racing boat and therefore most ketches you might look at are probably fairly heavily built.

The downsides are pretty much the same as the sloop, plus less performance to windward, more rigging to deal with and the smaller (mizzen) mast can get in the way of wind vane self steering.

The Yawl

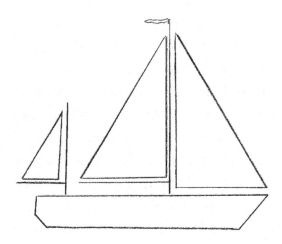

At first glance, the yawl looks fairly similar to the ketch. What differentiates them from a technical standpoint is the position of the smaller mast (the mizzen) forward or aft of the rudder post. In reality the mizzen of the yawl is a far less powerful sail than that of the ketch and is really only used to balance the larger forces of the forward part of the rig. What is interesting about them for us sea gypsies is that they have generally fallen out of favour with yachtsmen (for no good reason) and seem to fetch lower prices. I sailed on a Sparkman and Stephens yawl and it was as stiff as a church and went like a witch on a wakeboard whilst never feeling pressed or unbalanced.

The Junk Rig

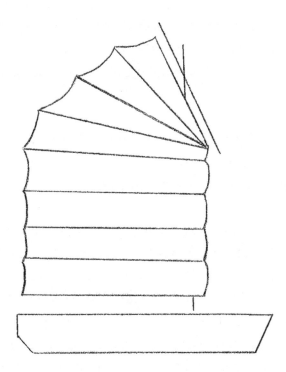

If you decide to go for the junk rig, then you will need to do some serious research because there have been many modifications in recent years. They are normally used in conjunction with freestanding masts, so you will have to satisfy yourself with those. I have no problem in theory with freestanding masts – they have proved themselves over and over again and can be very economical as there is no standing rigging to replace. However, some are made from carbon fibre, which whilst very strong and light, can become extremely weak if they have been hit by lightning and outrageously expensive, if not impossible to replace. (I was considering a boat with 2 freestanding carbon fibre masts and got a quote for $35,000 each. If I now had to ship and import those into Tahiti I would have to sell a major organ on the black market just to pay the deposit). Many junk rigs have freestanding wooden masts and you will have to look very closely at these for all the usual problems that come with wood.

Sunbird Marine specializes in junk rigs with freestanding aluminium masts and many of these are worth a look as they are much easier to maintain and replace.

The junk rig can make an excellent cruising rig. It is easy to handle, easy to reef, easy to maintain and the sails can be built by anyone with the right sewing machine, as they do not rely on complicated camber in order to function. Furthermore, they are fantastic off the wind (which is where you are most likely to be going) and do not require any specialist poles or sails to go dead downwind either. The price you pay for all these advantages is a reduction in windward performance and even this is being addressed by sail designers and by the addition of small jibs.

I am not an expert on the junk rig, but they seem to offer a lot for the budget-minded sea gypsy and everyone I know who has one is passionate about it. Google the Junk Rig Association for more info.

The Gaff Rig

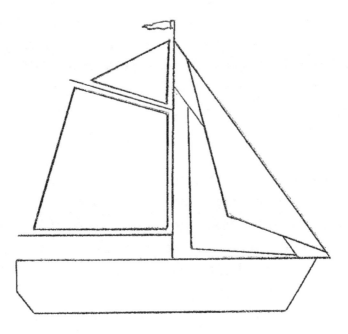

This is another rig that has fallen out of favour for no good reason. However, you rarely see them for sale and they might be a tad too complicated for your first boat. If you are inspired to buy one (and I totally see why), there is no good reason not to go for it, but be prepared to do a bit of studying and practising!

The gaff rig is a low-tech rig with a short-ish mast and imparts much less strain to the hull than the Bermudan rig. The gaff rig can fly a lot of sail up high (where the wind is) and is capable of some pretty decent performance. The masts tend to be spreader-less, so that you can square the mainsail off for good downwind performance. As the mainsail is square-ish (rather than a triangle) it does not pull the centre of effort forward when you reef it and subsequently heaves-to very well indeed (more on that later). The most famous modern exponent of the gaff rig is New Zealand sailor Nick Skeats. You can hear what he has to say about his Gaff rigged *Wylo II* on http://www.voyagingyachts.com/newwylo35.5/rig

Sails

All rigs need sails of course. Wind is going to be your main source of power, so try and get good ones and always have spares and a good repair kit. There are all kinds of high-tech sails out there and I am sure they are great (they better be for what they cost!). For the sailor on a budget, they can be largely ignored. Just about everyone I have ever met who is living on a boat uses dacron sails. Dacron is tough, UV resistant and has proved itself again and again.

If you are fixing up your boat in an area that has many yachts, used sails can often represent the best value. Many racing sailors change their sails each season and they are still perfectly efficient for our purposes. In La Paz (a bit of a Mecca for yachtsmen) we bought a virtually new Quantum mainsail and a never-used lightweight nylon drifter for a third of the new price and we are still using them today. New Zealand, Australia, the US and the UK all have commercial used sail lofts - all easily located by a quick internet search.
Try and go for the newest and heaviest dacron you can afford. Battens help with the sail shape, but you can live without them. All mainsails must have at least three reefing points.

You will have to watch out for this as many racing sails only have two reef points as racing sailors have no intention of ever heaving-to (more on that later). If you don't have a third reef, this essential technique will not be available to you in high winds unless you have a dedicated storm trysail. A storm trysail is a great thing to have and if your budget allows it, go and get one. Because our boat heaves-to so well, we simply use the third reef in our 10oz Dacron mainsail to heave-to, but I would like to have a dedicated storm trysail one day if Santa is listening.

On most rigs, the shape of the sail is important as this is where it derives its power. Old sails that have lost all their shape will still work fine downwind, but are hopeless to windward, so are generally to be avoided.

Sails for most rigs are complicated to build and require special tools. This is one area that even the most budget-minded sea gypsy is at the mercy of the marine professional. If you have bought a junk rig boat, the shape of the sail is not so critical and you can make them yourself out of virtually anything strong and UV resistant. Junk rig enthusiast and author Annie Hill uses Sunbrella (a registered trademark) to make her junk sails. Sunbrella is the material you see used for shade covers. It is relatively cheap, easy to work with and comes in some wild patterns too - so you could make some truly funky sails that reflect how happy you are to be going sailing without subsidising the piano-shaped swimming pool of yet another marine professional.

To reiterate though, this is not really a subject to get too hung up about (unless you find it interesting) as all the above rigs have their strengths and you will learn to make the best of them as you sail.

Chapter 6

Getting Real About Steel

The majority of boats you will see for sale are made from fibreglass (or 'frozen snot' as legendary designer Francis Herreschoff rather dismissively referred to it). Despite Mr Herreschoff's reservations, fibreglass has proved to be a very good, low maintenance boat building material when used correctly. When properly laid up and with sufficient thickness, fibreglass has a lot to recommend it.

However, some fibreglass boats are made so thin and light (in the tiresomely endless quest for speed and profit) that they are more suitable for storing bleach than for long term voyaging. Fortunately for us, these boats nearly always have narrow fin keels and spade rudders, making them fairly easy to spot. Some lighter fiberglass hulls are made with an inner core of wood or a high tech substance like Nolex. On an older boat, these are best avoided as repairing them can be complicated and the designer obviously had speed at the top of his wish list rather than longevity. This type of boat notwithstanding, a strong argument could be made for thick, well laid-up, solid fibreglass being the best hull material for a budget voyager.

Fibreglass is fairly strong, does not suffer from corrosion and can be moulded into some beautiful shapes. It can be ignored with fewer repercussions than other materials. There are certainly more fibreglass boats on the market than boats of any other material, making it the number one choice for most sea gypsies (including ourselves).

Steel boats, by contrast do not share the same low maintenance reputation and the internet is full of warnings about corrosion and pictures of badly made steel boats that look like the portable toilets at a grunge festival. However, much has changed recently in the world of steel and it might be worth a quick peek before we write it off completely.

Steel boats have always had their admirers and I include myself amongst them. They are strong and ductile (they will deform on impact without breaking), they are stiff and can absorb loads from rigging and waves crashing on the deck, they are fairly easy to repair in a developing country and you can run aground in them with less problems. (You meet the nicest people when you run aground, perhaps because only those with a highly developed sense of empathy stop to help you).

Yet many people are wary of steel boats because as anyone who has owned a car will know, steel can rust quickly in water and very quickly in a mixture of salt and water.

Three things have conspired in recent years though, to make steel a very viable option for the modern sea gypsy.

Coatings

Today's modern 2 part epoxy coatings have changed the way we see steel forever. Far more effective than any of the previous coatings, epoxy is easy to apply and virtually indestructible —providing a strong, waterproof barrier to the sea and therefore, corrosion.

Design

When steel was first used in cruising yacht design, the designs leaned heavily on the practices of traditional wooden boat builders. The ribs would be lofted and the steel plates welded on the sides. This lead to some very ugly boats indeed. Some were 'boxy' to say the least and others looked like half-starved horses (where the plates deformed between the ribs due to bad welding practices). Furthermore, it is well known that metal boats tend to rust from the inside out because little pockets of water get trapped where you can't see them - often where the ribs join the plates.

Fortunately there are steel boat designers like EG Van de Stadt and Brent Swain who use frame-less designs for their steel boats, all but eliminating this problem and making some nice looking boats into the bargain. Our last boat was a steel Van de Stadt 34 (pictured on the cover). She was nice looking, as strong as an ox in shin pads and we were very pleased with her.

Fear

People are unduly terrified of steel boats and this can work to the advantage of the wily sea gypsy with shallow pockets and big dreams, because less demand means lower prices. When we bought our steel Van de Stadt 34, she was practically new. We bought her for the price of the engine, mast and sails. If she had been made from fibreglass, we could never have afforded her.
Whenever you see a comparison between steel and fibreglass in the yachting press or in forums, they invariably come down on the side of fibreglass. These comparisons are inaccurate

because they tend to compare say, a new fibreglass hull with a new steel hull or a 5 year old fibreglass hull with a 5 year old steel hull under the misguided idea that this gives a fair comparison. These studies are made with the underlying assumption that money does not matter. Yet for us sea gypsies, money (or rather, value for money) is a reality we cannot ignore.

Confused?

Okay, for a really fair comparison between steel and fibreglass boats, you need to talk about cost, not age. For example we bought a practically new 34 foot steel boat for $50,000. Now compare this with a fibreglass boat that cost the same. There is no comparison. The same boat in fibreglass would be at least 20 years old, with a 20 year old diesel and other equipment. It is much more likely to have been in a collision than a practically new boat or repaired badly in some areas. Steering gear, winches, sails etc., are also 20 years old and there is probably some osmosis. A comparison based on cost would nearly always come down in favour of steel (except in Northern Europe, where steel boats fetch higher prices than elsewhere).

While we are on the subject (soapbox) here are some more advantages of the newer steel boat:

Osmosis.

Steel boats do not suffer from this, older fibreglass boats often do and can cost tens of thousands to put right. Our steel boat did need a bottom job (due to a stray electrical current that was easily detected and remedied) when we bought her, but the whole sand-blasting and application of epoxy resin cost $2000. Seven years later she is still sailing on the same bottom.

Chain Plates.

The problems with joining rigging to fibreglass, wood or ferro-cement, is solved by using large steel plates known as 'chain plates' to spread the load. This requires drilling through the hull material. These chain plates invariably take on some salt water through the bolt holes, or where they exit the deck, and begin to corrode. At the very least they are a constant source of concern because they are often buried deep in the fibreglass and not easy to inspect. You don't have this problem with steel as it is strong enough to weld an eye directly onto the deck or hull sides.

Waterlogged Decks

Most fibreglass boats have cored decks. This is where the decks are made like a sandwich – fibreglass as the bread with plywood or balsa as the filling. On older boats these are often waterlogged as they have absorbed sea and rainwater over the years through gaps in the deck fittings. Not a problem for steel decks.

Hull to Deck Joints.

Often a constant litany of leaks particularly (but not exclusively) in lightly built boats. In a steel boat, the process of welding usually results in a watertight deck to hull joint.

UV damage.

Many fibreglass boats show signs of 'crazing' particularly on the decks. Steel is unaffected by UV

Sailing.

A Bermudan rig has only one advantage over other types of rig and that is its increased ability to go to windward. To make the most of this, a bar-tight forestay is required. I would not feel comfortable applying such a constant high load to most fibreglass boats used for cruising and therefore much of the advantage of the Bermudan rig is lost on many fibreglass boats. A steel boat absorbs these loads without complaint.

Communication.

Another reason I like steel boats is that they speak to you. If there is anything that needs your attention your boat will produce a little brown weep of rust to show you where it is. (NOTE: this will do you no good at all if you cannot inspect every part of your boat because some crazy builder has covered the steel in teak or non-removable furniture!).

Fibreglass can slowly delaminate underneath the paint without any warning at all. In the picture below, water has slowly crept in around a through-hull fitting and delaminated the fibreglass over a number of years. I only discovered this when routinely removing the through-hull fitting for inspection. During removal, a whole section of fibreglass came away, still attached to the fitting!

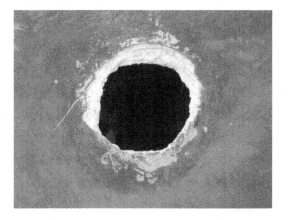

Lightning Protection

It may seem counter-intuitive, but steel boats are safer in thunderstorms by acting like a giant Faraday Cage (google it) which protects not only the people on board, but can help limit damage to your electrical goodies too.

Survival

Not an insignificant point. You are going to feel like the biggest smarty-pants in the world when you return to port safely with a boat that looks like a banana. The type of impact that would cause a steel boat to deform in this way would sink a boat of any other material.

Everything Else

Because the price differential means that everything else on the newer steel boat will be that much less used, just about anything you can think of, from rudder bearings to toilet seals, from rigging screws to radios, from diesel engines to sewage tanks is going to give you far less trouble (and therefore less money to spend) than the older fibreglass boat approaching a re-fit. This was certainly the case for us.

The newer steel boat (of frameless design and with the above caveats) is starting to look like not such a bad idea - even if you do have to keep an eye on the rust. (Remember, every inch of a steel boat must be inspectable!) Make sure you employ a surveyor who is accustomed to looking at steel boats because there are some dogs out there. He will probably have an audio gauge (a device that uses sound to measure the thickness of the steel) and another device for measuring stray current (a big enemy for all boats, but particularly steel and aluminium). Avoid all boats that have wood laid over the steel.

Also, you may want to learn to weld

Chapter 7

Getting a Good Deal – the Art of Negotiation

The man who lies to himself and listens to his own lie comes to such a pass that he cannot distinguish the truth within him.
Fyodor Dostoevski. The Brothers Karamazov

We are funny things us human beings. We find it hard to look rationally at virtually anything. Instead, we decide we want something (deep down in our lizard brain) and then go to extraordinary lengths to justify our decisions to ourselves. Before I became a wanderer on the sea, I had my own horse riding stable in Andalucia. Working for me briefly was an extremely beautiful young Canadian woman called Hayley. Unfortunately, Hayley was also as dumb as you can get and actually still remember to breathe. Various clients came and went during Hayley's short tenure and a number of my friends visited for extended periods. There would always be one who fell for beautiful Hayley. Do you know what they all had in common? The first thing they would say to me about their lustful feelings was:

"You know, that Hayley is not as dumb as she looks" or,

"Hayley is really quite deep when you get to know her" or some such twaddle like that.

Having worked with her and despite finding her very likeable, I can confirm that not only were these statements untrue, but Hayley was in fact, even dumber than she first appeared. Yet this opening statement would always mark the 'self justification' period of a person's infatuation with a painfully attractive ingénue.

Hayley was a wonderfully nice person otherwise and it is perfectly understandable why anyone would be attracted to her. Yet, ashamed that they were reacting to Hayley's physicality only, those that fell under her spell seemed to need to justify their physical attraction to her with something more noble.

The reason that I am boring you with this tale of lusty men and attractive idiots is that this is an extremely common human reaction and he or she who masters it, masters negotiation. Marketing types and brokers have an almost instinctual ability to recognize this trait and allow us to hang ourselves with it. The really good brokers don't 'sell' at all, but look for signs that you have seen a boat that your lizard brain likes and is now trying to justify to your rational brain. They then join you in this rationalization game to eradicate any doubts you might have. To a really good broker, the right boat for you is not the one that you need, but the one your lizard brain wants. In short, do not rely on the broker to talk you out of the wrong boat or into the right one.

At the risk of being repetitive, you must not fall in lust with the wrong boat and then justify that choice to yourself. The only way to ensure that you don't get sucked into this whole game is to educate your lizard brain so that you are genuinely attracted to the right boat and this is what this book is largely hoping to achieve. So, hopefully you will be able to spot the right boat without any further help, but just in case, here are some good shopping and negotiation tips:

Follow the guidelines in this book and walk away from anything on the 'not on my watch' list, despite what the salesman and other sailors might say. Be very wary about the things on the 'not ideal' list. Read the titles on the recommended reading list at the end of this book. These are written by real sea gypsies and yacht designers, not moneyed retirees or frustrated A-type personalities who still need to have the biggest and the best or fastest, way past the time they should have grown out of it.

Enjoy looking at boats! Boat buying is actually fun. Accept this and you won't want the process to stop. Once you have a boat, you will miss having a nosey around other people's yachts. Enjoy it! It is a buyers' market and there will always be a better one around the corner.

Do not use a surveyor who is recommended by the broker. Now, I am not saying that they are dishonest. I know many surveyors who go about their business with the best of intentions and will not give you a different survey simply to keep good relations with the broker. However, you have to put yourself in the position of the broker. If you were a broker, would you continue to recommend a surveyor who continually threw a spanner in your deals? Of course not. Make sure you get the number of the broker's recommended surveyor so that you can ignore him and engage somebody else.

Never be afraid to put in a low offer 'subject to sea trial and survey' and then reduce that offer further once the survey has found some problems (all boats have them).

I have a way of putting in a low offer that allows the seller to justify letting me have the boat at a good price: If the seller is asking $50,000 and I like the boat, I will offer $40,000 subject to sea trials and survey. The sea trial doesn't cost me anything, so I have that first. If happy with the sea trial, I order a survey (normally around the $600 mark). Once the survey comes back with all the problems (and all boats have 'em). I DO NOT go back to the broker and say "this yacht is a piece of shit".

Rather, I sit down and add up all the work needed to put the boat right, at top professional labour costs (including the things I have no intention of fixing). Hopefully, that should come to a nice sum (say $10,000) and return to the broker disappointed and dejected.

At his point I would like to stop you. While most brokers are friendly and nice, never forget that as far as buying the right boat at the right price is concerned, your relationship with your broker is at worst adversarial, at best a conflict of interests. The broker always takes her commission from the seller. Therefore, the broker is working for the seller. You cannot confide in your broker. For example, you cannot say,

"You know what? I like the boat, but let's try a lower offer and see if he goes for it", mistakenly believing that she will fight your corner with the seller. Whatever your broker hears from you will get back to the seller. The message the seller will get is,

"He likes the boat and has made a lower offer, but I think if you push him, he will come back up".

Whatever your broker believes about you, is what the seller will hear. So that is why I confide to the broker only those things that I want the seller to hear.

Okay, back to the story. I return to the broker dejected and when they ask how the survey went, I give them the bad news and my cost sheet to get it all fixed and explain that, while I love the boat, I will probably not be able to afford to go ahead with the deal due to all the money it will take to fix the problems.

"Give me a few days to think about it", I always say.

This gives the broker time to explain the situation to the owner (who has almost certainly started spending the money, at least mentally) and allows the owner the opportunity to digest the significance of the large amount of problems with the boat, whilst adjusting to the fact that the sale will probably fall through.

Now my fellow potential sea gypsy friends, there are a number of things working in your favour at this point. One is that people who want to sell a boat are disinclined to put any further money or time into it. The other is that boats cost money to keep, even when the owner isn't using them and this being a buyers' market, boats can easily rack up thousands of dollars being kept nice and pretty in the marina for prospective buyers to look at. In a few days, I will contact the broker tell them how much I love the boat, but the best I can do is 32k 'as is' due to all the work that is needed and my lack of funds ('as is' or 'as is, where is' are particularly important terms to know from the legal standpoint of buying a boat. They both mean that you will accept the boat in her current condition and all responsibility for fixing her up and/or moving her).

Now, as the owner was in the process of adjusting to the disappointment of a lost sale and contemplating a bill of at least $10,000 to get a clean survey (with no guarantee of a sale at the end of it), a whole bunch of hassle and several more months of payments for the marina, he is usually going to be happy with that. You of course, will do all the repairs yourself for a fraction of the cost of the marine professional and you have just got yourself a bargain.

I would add here, that this is in no way a rip-off. Why should you not get paid the same as a marine professional to put the boat right? I guarantee you will take longer and do a better job than most, simply because it is your life on the line. If you decide not to fix some things (wind direction indicators are a good example) that is your prerogative. The advertised price was based on a wind direction indicator that worked and you should not have to pay for one that does not.

I would also like to add that I never insult the owner, his yacht or come across as 'hardball'. That is for the movies. To get a good price, you must not anger the seller, you must engage him. You must never say things like:

"This boat is crap and it will cost 10k to fix, so here is 30k, take it or leave it". This will just get everybody's back up. Nobody likes to feel they have been muscled. No, your approach should be more like:

"I really love the boat and would really appreciate it if you could help me out here with a price reduction so that I can fix her up as I am not a rich man".

That is much more likely to get you what you want than a macho approach, as it allows the seller to justify the sale in his mind as 'doing you a favour'. Also, being friends with the previous owner will save you hundreds of dollars in wasted time and expense, as he is the best source of info you will ever have. Offer to take him sailing when the boat is fixed up. Make him a big lunch and spoil him with good wine. You might even make a friend. We did! We still email the previous owners of *Calypso* regularly with updates and they have been a mine of useful info and tips.

Dealing Direct with the Owner

While most boats seem to be for sale with brokers these days, creating a win/win environment is especially important when dealing directly with the seller and can often be more difficult than going through a broker. Sellers systematically over-value their own boats and often do not have the guiding hand of the market-savvy broker to point this out. Having said that, there are some real opportunities out there buying directly from the seller upon whom time and reality have had the appropriate effect – particularly because they are not losing 10 or 15 % to the broker. Most of the bargains will have been for sale for a while and be a bit seedy. Much depends on your willingness to fix them up, but a boat that is worth $30,000 in good condition that has gone a bit seedy and needs say $10,000 spent on her should sell for significantly less than $20,000 – otherwise, why not buy a boat that does not need so much of your input? There would be no point and the market recognizes that. In many ways, the shiny perfect boat in the marina can often be the least good value, but you will have to do the sums yourself, as each boat is different.

Another thing you will have to be aware of when dealing direct with the owner is the romance. He will no doubt, have a number of stories about the great times he has had aboard her and this will sell the boat to you. But these good times are not his to sell. This is just the reality of owning a good sailboat. Any good sailboat will give you those good stories, but things get cross-wired in the circuits of the human mind and you may end up associating those good times with this particular sailboat and see her value as greater than it really is.

Finally, never ask, "Why are you selling her?"

This is a pointless question, the answer to which is nothing more than an invitation for the seller or broker to help you with the self-justification process. Obviously you are interested in the boat and want to assure yourself that the owner is not selling her because she is a frightful old tub. If she is indeed a frightful old tub, the owner/broker will not say so - what you will hear instead is something to help you justify the boat in your mind (such as, 'he is retiring from sailing' or, 'she has a baby on the way') whether it is true or not.

Much better not to ask at all.

For a clearer picture, disengage your lizard brain and use your own senses or the cold, unbiased advice of a friend or surveyor, rather than rely on stories from the seller or his agent. In general, one must develop the self- awareness to know whether one is asking a question in order to truly find out the answer, or simply to give the seller the opportunity to sell your rational mind an idea that has already gripped your lizard brain. Go ahead and chase Hayley if you want to, but don't sell yourself the idea that she is smart in order to justify your lust.

Chapter 8

The Devil you Know – Getting Real About Risk

Blaming bad weather for boat losses is like blaming gravity for plane crashes.

Me. Just now.

More people are killed every year by falling coconuts than by sharks. Yet when we are having a tropical beach holiday do we look upward for coconuts, or do we hear that ominous semitone from the unforgettable *Jaws* movie theme?

Our perception of risk (like much of human intuition) is very skewed and not to be trusted. We process and become comfortable with many high-risk activities, whilst being petrified by other, fairly low risk activities. We get into the faux coziness of our cars (despite the risks being outrageously high) without a worry, yet most people are at least a little nervous just before their plane touches down (despite the risks being extraordinarily low). Over the last fifty years, fear of flying has diminished as we have had time to process the risk. When air travel was first thrust upon the general public, vast numbers of passengers were filling the puke bags as the fear of the new overwhelmed them. Now that air travel has become more assimilated into our consciousness, puke bags are hardly ever used. I am surprised they still have puke bags at all, particularly on short holiday flights. Health and safety would probably be better served if they filled them with free condoms.

90

The point is that we humans need time to process risk. There is no way around it, it cannot be bought and you can't pay someone else to do it for you. You *can* speed the process up a bit though.

In my previous life as a dirt dweller, I taught many people to ride horses. Most beginners are a little nervous and quite rightly so. This is a big, powerful animal that can buck you and kick your butt into next Tuesday without breaking a sweat. A horse killed Superman, a horse can kill you.
Furthermore, the beginner has no idea when or why the animal will do this or what the warning signs are. To make matters worse, the 21st century bombardment of news and media ensures that any bizarre accident involving horses is constantly available on YouTube or Facebooked endlessly for our ghoulish entertainment. Thusly, when a student arrives for her first lesson (a miracle in itself) she is usually far more nervous than is appropriate to the actual level of risk (particularly because I have a 100% safety record. Not relevant, just boasting).

So I approach new riders very differently than most riding stables, by starting with how to stop. I make the student practice these motions on a wooden horse until they are second nature. I then take my best behaved horse and sit the new rider on his back. I clip another line to the horse and walk in front of him, encouraging the horse to walk forward while the student tries to stop him. We do this for several lessons – increasing the speed the horse is allowed to achieve before the brakes are applied - until the student can stop the horse at jogging pace in a controlled manner without screaming and going foetal (which is most people's natural reaction and unfortunately, encourages the horse to go faster). I then spend sometime teaching the emergency dismount. Now the student is ready to learn the finer points of riding. Only once the student knows that she has a certain level of control and can bail out if necessary, can she reduce her fear levels to a point that will make the rest of the information sink in at a decent rate.

This is what you must do with your sailboat. You will not lose your fear without time and effort, but that time and effort must be spent first learning where the brakes are. Even if you are a real tough guy who craps bullets and laughs in the face of death, your partner will love you for this.

The Brakes

Reefing

Reefing is the action of reducing sail and slowing the boat down. When the wind pipes up, it is very rare that the wind itself is the problem. Some sailors even say that there is no such thing as too much wind, only too much sail. I am not sure if I totally agree with this, but there is a certain amount of truth in the fact that an important part of keeping your boat under control is having an appropriate amount of sail up for the amount of wind blowing. It is beyond the scope of this book to cover all the different reefing systems, but you must learn to do this on your boat quickly, efficiently and without panic. All boats are different and you will have to practice, practice, practice this skill until it is second nature.

Here are the two most important tips about reefing:

1) If you think you might need a reef, you do need a reef. Don't wait. Do it now.

2) If you can still make forward progress, then take a reef in before dark. If the wind is too light to allow this, then keep a VERY weather eye open.

Heaving-to

One of the most important 'brake' skills you must learn is a practice that many sailors have forgotten. That practice is called 'heaving-to' and is not only an essential storm tactic, but also a way of buying yourself time when things are going wrong or when you simply need to take a break. Practice this technique and you will always know where the brakes are.

The best and most exhaustive description of how to heave-to can be found in *Storm Tatics* by Lin and Larry Pardey, which I strongly advise you to buy (see recommended reading or visit our website). However, here in a nutshell is how you do it. I am assuming that you are already on deeply reefed sails.

1. Turn your boat into the wind and sheet your mainsail to the centre so that she stops making forward progress.

2. Roll in your headsail(s)

3. Lash the tiller or wheel so that the rudder is turning you into the wind naturally without tacking. (The ideal is about 50 degrees off the wind, but if you are practising in winds of less

than 30 knots, do not be too disappointed if you only get about 65 degrees. Once the wind pipes up, it helps)

All boats are different and you will struggle with this manoeuvre if you have ignored my advice earlier in the book and bought a fin keel/spade rudder boat, but even such a bad choice of boat can be made to heave-to with a little extra fiddling about. If your boat tries to tack, then leave a bit of headsail up and allow it to back-wind. If the boat falls off the wind too much, take in all headsail, point the boat more to windward and tighten up the mainsheet. Go and experiment – you'll soon get the hang of it. If you have bought a ketch or a yawl (two masted boat with the aft mast being smaller - see chapter 5), this is where they really shine, but any good, longish-keeled boat should heave-to nicely.

That's it! This will settle your boat like a duck snoozing in the water with its bill tucked under its wing. You will be amazed how calm everything becomes. You are now free to go below, have a little cry (you won't be the first) or a cup of tea and think clearly about whatever ails you. I always do this if the crew are looking nervous in order to calm everyone down. The biggest empire the world has ever seen was built on decisions delayed by tea and I am beginning to see why. Tea does not give you super powers (well, except a really good Darjeeling which makes you invincible) but it does slow you down and stop you doing anything stupid. The quality of your decisions will improve and your crew will be happy. Heaving-to is a sailor's magic safety valve and can transform your sea gypsy experience.

Perhaps the most amazing thing about heaving-to is how

many sailors don't know how to do it or don't believe it works. I put this largely down to misinformation.

You will read an awful lot of rubbish written about heaving-to by 'respected' sailors. You can't blame them. They have read a lot of rubbish written by other 'respected' sailors. Treat it all with a large pinch of salt. There are two reasons that many sailors are quick to dismiss heaving-to. The first is quite simple, the second, a little darker.

The first is easy to explain: If you have ignored the advice in this book and bought exactly the kind of boat that is not designed to be in rough weather (as most people seem to) then you can hardly be surprised when the techniques that work on proper sea boats don't work so well on your air conditioned, double-glazed yoghurt pot. But rather than kick themselves for buying a wholly inappropriate boat, the owners blame the technique of heaving-to (despite the fact that it has saved more seamen than a teenager's bedsheets)[6].

The second reason is that the most well-known sailors are racing sailors, and to understand their mentality we need to dip into the world of yacht racing and the coverage it receives by a media that can't tell the difference between a Pit Bull Terrier and a Labrador.

---

[6] In Lin and Larry Pardey's excellent book *Storm Tactics,* there is a quote from veteran Coast Guard rescue swimmer Mario Vittone. Mr Vittone says, *"In my line of work, I have pulled dozens of people off their boat for the last time. Never have I seen (or heard of) anyone needing rescue from a vessel that was properly hove-to with or without a para anchor".* The key words here are 'never' and 'properly'. If you have followed the advice in this book, you already have a boat that will heave-to 'properly'. Wouldn't it be great to practice the technique until the word 'never' also applied to you?

Pit Bull Terriers and Racing Yachts

(Stay with me on this)

It seems that not a week goes by without somebody being attacked by a Pit Bull Terrier. In fact, at the time of writing another man (this time in Indiana, USA) has been chomped to death by the family pet. A very sorry affair all round which has led to calls for Pit Bulls to be banned.

Because most of us have at least some basic knowledge of the differences between dog breeds, we can see that this is an issue for this one type of dog (and possibly one type of owner) and does not apply to dogs as a whole which as we all know, are generally little fluffy bundles of love.

The same logic can be applied to yachts.

Potential sea gypsies need to be at least as aware of the differences between types of yacht as they are breeds of dog. This will significantly help with the process of understanding, reducing and assimilating the level of risk involved, as well as demonstrating why a large pinch of salt has to generally accompany much of the advice or techniques advanced by racing sailors (and particularly where the subject of heaving-to is concerned).

The last time I was in Australia, I saw a documentary about the sinking of the racing yacht *Excalibur*, which overturned killing 4 crew and occasioning a massive rescue operation[7].

---

[7] *Australia Story* ABC Television.

All the contributors were keen to point out that the reason the boat overturned was faulty welding on the keel, which had dropped off. Did anyone see the photographs of the upturned boat with the keel stub protruding? Well, one does not have to be a disaster engineer (although I am actually a disaster engineer) to see that, unlike traditional seaworthy designs where the keel is connected along the centreline of much of the hull, this keel was attached to about 8% of it. Imagine a horizontal baguette with a pencil shoved in the bottom and you have more or less got it. This type of keel cuts drag but concentrates enormous forces where the keel joins the hull and all points close by. Had the boat been designed with a more seaworthy keel, a bit of faulty welding would have gone unnoticed.

The first problem (and from which many others flow) is design motivation. Whether it comes from selective breeding in the case of the pit bull terrier, or the designer's board in the case of a racing yacht, many of these so-called accidents can be traced back to a questionable decision at the concept level.

In the case of the pit bull, it is easy to see the process: redneck owners like aggressive dogs to hunt wild pigs. Rather than suggest counselling to the owner, the breeder selects increasingly aggressive dogs until this aggression makes them unstable and overflows into an attack on a human, which inevitably (and quite rightly) leads to the calling for stricter controls on this type of dog. We all understand this process, but this simple logic is largely overlooked when a yacht accident occurs. When a racing yacht goes down it is *yachts as a whole* which get tarred as 'dangerous' rather than racing yachts and racing mentality.

Yacht racing, motor sport, skiing (and indeed most sports) are hives of innovation. Weight ratios are tweaked, streamlining is honed, new materials and technologies are constantly being examined, all in order to shave a few seconds off a given course. And what great fun it is watching Casey Stoner clip one tenth of a second from Valentino Rossi or Lewis Hamilton streak home in first place from way back in the Formula 1 grid. Of course there are accidents and yacht racing is no different. Or at least that is the received wisdom.

In fact, nothing could be further from the truth.

Yacht racing differs enormously from other sports in two fundamental ways.

Racing Design

Designing racing yachts, like racing cars, is mostly a matter of reducing weight and drag while increasing power. This has led to the sacrifice of seaworthiness in the pursuit of speed. Hulls have become thinner, keels deeper and overly stressed, masts taller. Generally, a racing yacht is designed for the type of conditions normally to be encountered rather than those that might be encountered. Any yacht designed to weather the type of seas that only occur rarely will not be competitive in normal conditions. It is the equivalent of designing a Formula One car with suspension heavy enough to cope with a deep pothole. Why drag the extra weight around?

However, a formula one track is entirely predictable and

manageable and there is no need to prepare for something as unlikely as a pot-hole. Offshore, the ocean is most certainly NOT predictable and designers who pretend otherwise are at best, giving sailing a bad name and at worst, criminally negligent.

The fate of the *Excalibur*, was as much due to the triumph of speed over seaworthiness in design as it was to faulty welding. The sea is not Brands Hatch or Monte Carlo, there are no paramedics standing by on every corner if your super-fast, ultra-light vessel has a problem. The sea is a problem – a constant stream of them. Weather will occasionally overstress the boat, whales do collide with keels, helmsmen do make mistakes and tradesmen do occasionally take less pride in their work than one might hope; and if you are a skipper acting as if that is not true in the pursuit of speed and glory, then you do not deserve the name. You certainly do not deserve to have the brave men and women of the Coast Guard risk their neck at the tax-payers' expense to bail you out.

Racing Mentality

On that same visit to Australia I also saw the sad images of the racing yacht *Shockwave V* broken upon the rocky shore of Flinders Islet, with two crew lost - including legendary Aussie sailor, Andrew Short. The boat was taking part in the 92 nautical mile Flinders Islet Race, which starts in Sydney Harbour, rounds Flinders Islet and returns to Sydney.

In the climate of grief, it is easy not to ask the obvious question: How, in an age when we can compute our position to within a few meters, did this boat collide with the island it was supposed to be going around? The answer is of course, speed and ego. Clearly the skipper had miscalculated his position, maybe not by much, but enough to crash into a clearly charted Islet. If the skipper were miles away from the island (as any responsible skipper should have been on a dark night in a lumpy sea) instead of cutting it so fine in the name of victory, then a small error of position would have gone unnoticed and unpunished.

The point is that many racing skippers are too overly concerned with winning to be truly good captains. Excellent sailors they may be, but a captain's first responsibility is the safety of all the souls onboard, not to obsess about the little thrill he is going to give himself when he raises a cheap trophy back at the club. If a skipper is so concerned with winning that he neglects to take a wide berth around a clearly charted Islet, then how much less likely do you think he is to heave-to (which is basically stopping) to confirm his position or weather out a squall? Many racing sailors dismiss heaving-to as a tactic, not because it doesn't work, but because it slows them down.

So, what has all this got to do with pit bull terriers and sea gypsies? Well quite a lot actually. A pit bull terrier is a dog for hunting pigs, not for walking in the park. Racing design and mentality is suitable for inshore waters only where the course can be monitored to much the same level as the Monaco Grand Prix. Taking a racing yacht or racing mentality into the open sea is akin to high speed bush-bashing in a formula one car – they are not designed for it and overly competitive skippers with A-type personalities will only make that fact more obvious as they attempt to put their name on another trophy.

Yes, there is some risk in sailing, but it is probably less than you think. You are not going to buy a super-light racing machine. You are going to buy a good sea boat that heaves-to properly and does not punish small mistakes or construction faults with catastrophe. You are not going to race, or even set yourself a goal other than arriving somewhere safely and enjoyably. You are certainly NOT going to risk the lives of your crew for the fleeting pleasure of holding a little trophy up in the yacht club and showing everyone what huge balls you have.

We have been so swamped with the image of a hero as a testosterone-fuelled, goal-orientated, risk-taking male ('one man alone against the mighty sea!') it has blinded us to the fact that the very absence of these qualities is the key to safety at sea and the mark of a good captain. You cannot 'beat' the ocean, so don't fight it and don't be put off by the accidents caused by those who think they can.

Chapter 9

Show Me the Money

Only an unreconstructed hippy who has never been on a boat thinks the wind is free. It is not. But it can be quite good value. The cost of the wind is easy to calculate. Add up all of the miles you do on your boat and divide it by the cost of maintenance and depreciation.

For example, if you have spent $10,000 over the last five years and have travelled 5000 miles, the wind has cost you 2 bucks a mile. Of course, to get a really accurate figure, you have to estimate how much longer the stuff you bought will last and how much of what you spent was actually used to enhance the sailing of the boat (rather than say, a new sound system or diesel engine), but you can get a pretty accurate idea. Whatever your answer, it won't be zero.

Yet harnessing the wind is only one of the expenses a boat can give you and in many ways the least of your worries. There are bigger enemies to your gypsy budget, but the good news is that most of them can be avoided or controlled. Here are a few of the main culprits:

MARINAS

Excuse the capital letters – I used them because I am actually shouting and it is hard to get that across. If you want to be a sea gypsy, marinas must be avoided like Jehovah's Witnesses. When you pick your place in the sun to start your gypsy life, make sure there is a good anchorage or two nearby. Avoiding marinas is the key to the gypsy life and much more fun too.

Travelling around Australia in a camper van in 2007, I found the caravan parks there quite good value. For about $20US, you could get a nice big plot with water and electricity and often in lovely countryside. Yet $20 a day is still $620 a month, so I would often free-camp in the bush. Marinas are nothing like as cheap as camp-sites, they are more crowded and you don't even get free electricity at most of them any more.

Furthermore, the plot you get is almost non-existent, with your neighbours crushed up against you, window to window. In many marinas that use the 'med moor' system (i.e. you put an anchor out front and tie the stern to the dock) you are literally bounced off your neighbour every time a surge comes in. They are hot too, as the breeze gets stifled by all the boats and marina buildings.

Peace and quiet can also be an issue – your need for it as well as your need to ignore it when you fire up your power tools to fit a cabinet to your new floating home. In fact, many if not most, marinas explicitly ban working on your boat. On top of that, you cannot enter a marina without insurance (more on insurance later).

Marinas offer absolutely nothing to the sea gypsy except a fuel and water dock. They also vary wildly in price. The cheapest we ever stayed in was at Santa Rosalia in the Sea of Cortez which was $10 a day (This marina was so close to falling to bits, that despite being tied to the pontoon, we still set the anchor alarm as it looked as if the pontoon may detach itself and float out to sea at any minute. Absolutely charming though and managed with the kind of friendliness that is unfortunately in decline).

The most expensive was Cabo San Lucas (on the tip of Baja California). We didn't stay there (obviously), but were quoted $160 a day. The average for a 36 foot boat like ours is around $36 dollars (a dollar a foot). More in French Polynesia, less in Thailand and Malaysia.

Prices vary wildly, but a dollar a foot is a good rule of thumb. Most places add tax and electricity and a few charge for water too. However, even at $36 a day, you are still looking at over $1100 a month, which is a lot for most sea gypsies. For us, it is approaching twice our monthly budget, so you better get good at, and enjoy, life at anchor.

Oh life at anchor! What bliss compared to the constant crush and bustle of the marina! This lifestyle has so much more to offer than the showy marina life and it's free! For a start, you get to meet other sea gypsies who are just like you! Heaps of them. Let's face it folks, if you are reading this book, you are probably not rich and even if you are, you are the type of person who sees more value in honest friendship, honest sea boats and spiritual kinship than those whose main desire is to have the spunkiest boat in the marina and are prepared to work themselves to death for the title and the privilege of paying thousands each month just to park the ego (remember the price goes up with size!). Yes, living at anchor is far more than just cheap. Learn to be comfortable at anchor and you make a dream a possibility.

Marine Professionals

Take anything in the world - a light bulb, a bolt, a pulley, a dustpan and brush and put the word 'marine' in front of it and it miraculously doubles in price. The same goes for plumbers, carpenters, mechanics, electricians, riggers, even cooks. Take any third rate mechanic and add the word 'marine' to his business card and suddenly he is charging $100 an hour for doing what your local mechanic does for $30 and with virtually no expenses (the marine tradesman does not need expensive premises to attract customers or lift their cars up, just a lock-up garage with a few tools and a business card).

Fortunately, my background in horses actually prepared me for this because the same process is at work there too – add the word 'equestrian' to anything and the price hits the roof. Professional marketers call this 'price differentiation' – the technique of selling the same product at two different prices to two different markets.

Funnily enough, this process seems to work for exactly the same reason in horses as in the marine world. In both cases there is a massive split in the market. Horses seem to be owned by fairly well off people and dirt-poor farmers - and both have similar needs to be filled on wildly different budgets. Similarly there are some multi-million dollar yachts in the marina, whilst outside in the anchorage are all the sea gypsies.

I have noticed recently that prices for marine professionals are going up and up despite the economic hardships. This can only be because the rich continue to pay what they are asked because they have plenty of money and it is too much hassle ue.

I saw this process at work in Marina de La Cruz in Mexico. My friends who live in the marina (we of course were in the lovely anchorage outside) were complaining about (yet another) hike in the price of the berths. I suggested that they all come out to the anchorage for a week as a protest – to show the marina's management that enough is enough! Do you know how much support that idea got? Nada. Zip. www.buggerall.com.
The idea was met with an overwhelming wave of apathy.

"It's too much hassle."
"It's only 10%",
"Prices go up, they just do."
And all that kind of fatalistic nonsense.

Six months later, there was another price rise. That was paid as well.

The same thing is happening with marine professionals. You can't blame them though, it is just good capitalism. If you owned a hotel and successive price hikes had no effect on the occupancy rate, then wouldn't you keep putting the prices up until bookings started to tail off? The rich keep on paying and now marine professional services are sky high and too often below the standard of shore services.

One sail maker in Mexico wanted to charge me $60 an hour for two whole days of work ($960). Expensive enough already, but as we had actually been assisting on both those days, we knew for a fact that this old guy had spent more than 80% of the time he was billing us for, flirting with Jasna or showing us pictures of his old boats and telling spurious sea stories. You can imagine what I had to say about that! The expectation was that I would be happy to pay whatever I was asked, even though I was knowingly being cheated. After all, yachting is expensive and everybody likes to show off their wealth right?

Your money, like mine, probably took you a little while and some effort to earn and you have every right to expect other people to treat it with at least a little respect. I didn't earn it by charging $100 an hour for very little and I am not going to spend it with those that expect this kind of easy ride. And when a tradesman spends all day chasing after my wife, he better not even dream about being paid for it.

Now, the good news is that there are not one, but four silver linings in this toxic cloud of naked capitalism:

Firstly, you will be forced to work out how to do most things yourself and ultimately become a better seaman (the more you practice creative problem solving, the better you will be when you need to call on it).

Secondly, you will almost certainly develop some skills that you can then market to the rich folks on their big yachts to raise some cruising funds.

Thirdly, these ridiculous prices have given rise to a whole army of sea gypsies who work 'under the table' at competitive rates and sometimes for free or exchange. I have, just recently swapped some mechanical work for some rigging and made some cool friends into the bargain. In other cases, where the sailor did not have any skills that I needed at that time, I was happy to swap mechanical work for a good dinner and a couple of beers. If you don't have enough technical skills to swap, you can cook, clean, pull teeth – just about anything. The picture below shows Jasna having her hair cut in a boatyard by Kirsty of SV *Tigress,* who tops up her gypsy kitty with comb and scissors. Not only was this the cheapest and most convenient hair cut Jasna had ever had, it was also the best – probably because the sea gypsy community still relies heavily upon reputation. So if you see SV *Tigress* on your travels, perhaps it is time for that mohawk you always fancied.

Finally, avoiding marine professionals will force you to practice the language! Pretty much all those who want to part you from your cash will have some skill in English. For many, it is the only thing that gets them hired. An English speaking 'marine canvas expert' from the marina will talk to you about replacing your cushion covers for 'only' $500 dollars. Yet, a few streets back from the marina, there will be a little upholsterer's shop that will do it for $100. This guy cannot speak English, runs an honest business for local people and will probably do the best job too. As if that was not reason enough to choose a non-marine tradesman, you get to practice your language skills, meet local people and see how they live and often acquire some new friends in to the bargain.

I apologise to the few good tradesmen out there who do an honest job for reasonable money, but they are as endangered (and heading the same way) as giant pandas and polite doctors. Avoiding marine professionals is not just an essential part of controlling costs, but is also more spiritually rewarding in the long run. I mean, what adventures are you going to have if your only involvement in the life of your boat is to point to a problem, sign a cheque and say, "fix it"?

Furthermore, there will come a time when you are in the middle of dog-turd-nowhere, where there are no marine professionals or fancy chandleries, and you are going to have to start your engine using a rope and a local fishing boat (true story), fix your gearbox with a washer from a winch (still going strong 2 years later) or climb the mast to free up a jammed halyard (Jasna always does this because she likes to free her inner monkey).

If this is the first time you have tried to haul your bottom up the mast or used the creative problem solving part of your brain, then rather than feel confident about the challenge, you are going to experience fear, guilt (every rich skipper secretly suspects he should understand more about his boat than he actually does), pain and frustration. If you happen to be drifting towards a reef at the time, you may also experience shipwreck, bankruptcy, wet feet and more than a little embarrassment.

Some problems aren't solvable. Most are if you are accustomed to thinking a certain way and there is only one way to get that kind of experience and it does not involve money. In fact, the ability to pay somebody else to figure it out is a distinct disadvantage.

So, How Much Does it Really Cost?

The prize for the most ridiculous answer to this question (and there is an extraordinarily high level of competition for this accolade) goes to J P Morgan Senior, who answered with depressingly predictable snobbery,

"You have no right to own a yacht if you ask that question",

...thereby also nominating himself for the award of, 'World's Biggest Dick in Merchant Banking', which I believe to be an even more hotly contested title.

Juxtapose Mr Morgan's rather unfortunate attitude with what Hollywood actor Sterling Hayden had to say about the subject:

"To be truly challenging, a voyage, like a life, must rest on a firm foundation of financial unrest. Otherwise, you are doomed to a routine traverse, the kind known to yachtsmen who play with their boats at sea... "cruising" it is called. Voyaging belongs to seamen, and to the wanderers of the world who cannot, or will not, fit in. If you are contemplating a voyage and you have the means, abandon the venture until your fortunes change. Only then will you know what the sea is all about. "I've always wanted to sail to the south seas, but I can't afford it." What these men can't afford is not to go. They are enmeshed in the cancerous discipline of "security." And in the worship of security we fling our lives beneath the wheels of routine - and before we know it our lives are gone.
Sterling Hayden

A much better answer which could almost be the mantra of the sea gypsy. A little extreme for some tastes perhaps (it is nice to have *some* resources), but the point is a fair one. Chucking money at a voyage is easy, unrewarding and ultimately futile if you are in a part of the world where the services you want to buy do not exist. Nor does this attitude make you a better seaman or person. These qualities cannot be bought and are one of the many gifts that relative poverty is holding in its outstretched hand.

So how much is enough?

In the aftermath of the global financial crisis, we have hopefully learnt to be sceptical about virtually anything muttered by bankers, but even sailors can be a bit vague on the subject of money. Within the pages of some otherwise excellent sailing books, the authors are mysteriously coy about how much money they spend. I find many people are puzzlingly reticent to talk about money. They will bore you witless about the most intimate details of their lives (including their sex lives) but become blushing debutantes as soon as the ugly question of cash hoves into view.

Annie Hill's great book *Voyaging on a Small Income* explores her extremely lowly finances in great detail, but is hopelessly out of date and too extreme for many tastes. In their excellent book, *The Cost Conscious Cruiser*, Lin and Larry Pardey frequently share their great techniques for saving money. They also publish the budgets of people they know. But when it comes to what *they* are actually living on (which is all you can really know for sure because so many people are either shocking book-keepers or outright liars) they are strangely silent.

This tended to frustrate me when I was dreaming about sailing away forever because, let's face it, to engage fully in the subject we have to know that it relates to us – can we do it? Can we afford it? Do you want to pour your time and energy into researching something only to find out there is no way you can afford it? Perhaps it is vulgar to talk about money, but this was always my first question and I imagine it is yours.

So, to set the record straight, these are our most recent figures. If we averaged it out over three years instead of one, it would be higher because we were working on our boat. The reason we have not included those figures is because only you can know how much work your boat will need. It might not even need much, so including our fitting out costs in the final tally, might unduly scare you a bit, as we knowingly took on a boat that needed a bit of work because the price was right. Just for you to get an idea though, we bought our boat for $36,000 and spent $25,000 and a very leisurely 2 years sailing her around and preparing her while we earned money working.

Our Norwegian friends Tina and Oyvan on SV *Freya* bought their lovely 32 foot Bayfield cutter for $17,000 and were off sailing in less than a month with only a couple of thousand bucks in further expenses. Several friends of ours bought their boat for less than $10,000 and had them sailing locally for another $5000, so do not be put off if you have less money than we did. There are plenty of cheap boats out there that require more sweat than money.

What the figures below represent then, is how much it costs to keep going once you are set up. The figures include ongoing maintenance and replacement of stuff that has broken since the original fit-out.
However, all figures are useless unless you know what we are actually doing with our boat. If we sit in a free anchorage all year, eating beans, drinking cleaning products, never going out and not using the boat, then we would spend less money, but the figures would be less relevant to someone who intends to actually sail their boat and have fun. So firstly, here is what we did in the last year.

Number of Nights

At anchor: 283 (77%)
On passage: 50 (14%)
In the boatyard: 17 (5%)
On a mooring: 15 (4%)
In a marina: 0 (0%)
On land: 0 (0%)
Total sea miles: 4696
Longest passage: 32 days (Mexico – Marquesas)
Total days sailing: 86
Motoring hours: 167
Litres of fuel: 270 (twice our normal consumption. This was an unrepresentative year for engine use)

Money (in Euros)

April: 0
May: 331
June: 290
July: 592
August: 205
September: 1018
October: 1000
November: 293
December: 1034 (incl. new autopilot control head)
January: 411
February: 654
March: 666

Average 540 Euros per month for two people (270 each)[8]

---

[8] I have kept the figures in Euros, because at the time of writing, the US$ is enjoying a particularly high historical value against other currencies, which would skew the results and make life seem a little more expensive for those of us who do not own any. If you are coming from the USA, then you are in luck, because world travel has never been cheaper for you. Get real and get gone my American brothers and sisters! Before it all comes crashing down again.

In April we spent nothing as we were crossing the Pacific. Similarly, we were on passage most of November. August and September were quite high as we were making some repairs and provisioning in Tahiti. December was quite high because we bought a used autopilot control head on ebay to replace the one that drowned when a big wave came into the cockpit two days out of Mexico.

We have friends who live on less and those that live on more, but this is more or less what we spend, now that the boat has been fixed up. We are definitely in the budget end (we know more people with larger budgets than smaller ones) but by no means do we feel deprived. We eat well and drink well (we make our own wine on the boat) and have everything we need or want.

Because we chose a small boat, we do not worry about the sail ripping and costing ten grand to replace. We live a real dream life with few worries because for us, the most important thing is not how much you live on, but what that money represents, which brings us neatly to the next chapter and the philosophy at the core of the sea gypsy life.

Chapter 10

Sustainability

What does a man need - really need? A few pounds of food each day, heat and shelter, six feet to lie down in - and some form of working activity that will yield a sense of accomplishment. That's all - in the material sense, and we know it. But we are brainwashed by our economic system until we end up in a tomb beneath a pyramid of time payments, mortgages, preposterous gadgetry, playthings that divert our attention from the sheer idiocy of the charade.
The years thunder by, the dreams of youth grow dim where they lie caked in dust on the shelves of patience. Before we know it, the tomb is sealed.

Good old Sterling Hayden *again*

As I have said in the previous chapter, we have friends with larger budgets than ours, and friends who think our 540 Euros a month something of an extravagance. It is tempting to envy those with more money to spend and to have pity for those with less, but this is missing the point. The actual budget that you have is far less important than whether it is sustainable or not.

If your outgoings exceed your income, then you are going home – probably quite soon. If you cannot make enough money to pay your bills while you are out sailing, what other option is there? To be fair, many sailors set a certain amount of cash aside say, $10,000 a year for three years and that is what they spend. After the three years are up, they sell up, go home and go back to work. There is nothing wrong with this approach, but this is a book about sea gypsies who want to sail away forever and part of that philosophy is that we go where we want, when we want and without the hand of time pressing on our shoulder. If you have a year to get back to Plymouth before the money runs out and you are currently in the Solomon Islands, well that idea flies out of the window quicker than a Lehman Brothers accountant. You need to get cracking if you are going to get back to work and pay the mortgage!

What Jasna and I really adore about living on the sea is the pace of life. Very recently we went to a wonderfully idyllic little atoll in the south Pacific called Fakarava. Two days' sail north-east of Tahiti, Fakarava is truly one of the most beautiful places on Earth. We liked it so much we stayed for six weeks. The Whitsunday Islands off the coast of eastern Australia are so varied and spectacular, we wasted 6 months there. We liked Mexico so much, we stayed there for three years. (To be fair, this is where we chose to buy and renovate our current boat *Calypso*.- our 'place in the sun'. We could have been out in a year, but when you are somewhere as amazing as Mexico, where's the rush?).

We can do this, because time and money are no longer the same thing to us. Because our income now slightly exceeds our outgoings, we get (ever so slightly) richer every day by doing what we like to do.

Time is certainly NOT money.

I saw a news article on Australian TV a few years ago which claimed that the average Australian, should he lose his job, would be bankrupted by his credit payments within 3 weeks. I found that very hard to believe, so I asked around and surprisingly, found it to be true. Some of my friends said that they would not last a week - and these are people with good jobs!

The rising acceptance of debt as a way of life has given legs to the old adage 'time is money'. When you have to make thousands every month to pay the mortgage, car, school fees, furniture etc, then the pressure of meeting your payments can mask the madness of this way of living.

It is as if you are running down the tracks of your life, just staying barely ahead of the juggernaut of debt that is closing on your heels. You must keep running because the minute you trip or even ease up a bit, you are going to get squished flat. As you sprint ever onwards, it may occur to you that this is a crazy way to live, but you look around and everybody else seems to be running just ahead of their own juggernaut, so you imagine this is just part of life.

"Maybe", we think, "if I could just run a bit faster for a while and 'get ahead' then perhaps I could gain a bit of breathing room and slow the pace down a bit?"

So we run a bit faster, work an extra job, take risks driving too fast between those jobs, gamble on the stock market or even the betting shop. Even those who do nothing will often dream about having more money to put a little distance between themselves and their juggernaut of debt.

Perhaps it might be better to get out of the road and stop running altogether. Step on to the grass verge and let the juggernaut speed by. Sit down for a while. Breathe. Pick a flower. Time can go back to being just time if you follow a few simple rules.

Get rid of all debt. Give the car back (you won't be needing it) sell the house or rent it out if it shows positive cash-flow, pay off your credit cards and throw them away. Declare bankruptcy if you have to, but get rid of debt. This is the first move to becoming a sustainable sea gypsy.

Cut your expenses and live cheaply. Don't wait until you have bought a boat, do it now, while you are getting your funds together, so that all your resources can go into becoming a sea gypsy. Jasna and I lived in a cheap, shared house while we worked to get the money together for *Calypso*. She was 32 and I was 45, so we were the oldest people there, but it can be fun to be a student again!

Think in terms of income, rather than money. We have a few dollars tucked away in various funds, which pay us about 4% a year in interest. The rates are historically low at the moment and the average interest we have received over our eight years as sea gypsies is actually 6.6%. If you have a little nest egg from selling your house or a kidney, this can provide everything you need as a budget sailor. If you have a smaller nest egg, then it could still take the heat off. For example, say you have sold your house and resisted the urge to spend the proceeds on a massive status symbol. Instead, you have bought and fixed up your modest little proper sea-boat and have 200,000 Euros left over. Well, at an average of 6.6% interest, this will provide you with an income of 13000 Euros a year and because you bought a nice little sea gypsy boat you can sail off into the sunset forever and never touch the principal. Woo-hoo! Congratulations, you are sustainable!

However, just because most of us have nothing like that sum of money, this should not deter us from thinking in terms of income. Say you have managed to set off with a little left over or have saved up some money fixing diesel engines in Martinique. Maybe you have $20,000 and are thinking about buying a flash new chart plotter, a water maker and a freezer. Don't do it! A sea gypsy thinks not in absolute cash numbers but in income. Once that cash is spent on toys for your boat, it is gone. Whatever you buy will also need maintaining and therefore, of course, generate more expenses.
Invested at 6.6% that same money will provide 1320 Euros per year. Every year. Year in, year out. Ideally, it would be nice to put a little back in against inflation, so let's say 1200 Euro a year –that is 100 Euro a month. Forever. Even if you have only saved 5000 Euros, that is still 330 Euros a year (nearly 30 Euros a month). Forget about the 5000 Euro, what you have is 30 Euros a month and that is what you can spend.

Forget turning every windfall into toys or nights out. Resist the urge to go crazy when you arrive in your 'place in the sun' (certainly try not to spend your entire nest egg in the local brothel as a charming English guy we met in Mexico had done. He is now eeking out a living as a labourer and as soon as he gets a little coin, the brothel girls relieve him of it. At least he is supporting the local economy, I suppose). Instead, turn it into income and add the income to your budget. As your gypsy life progresses, you can add any extra money you make to this fund and your income will start creeping up. Your expenses will fall as you get better at budgeting and maintaining your boat, and before you know it, your income is outstripping your expenses! This extra income is what you can spend on luxuries. That is how a sea gypsy thinks and the very definition of 'sustainable'.

This topic and philosophy is covered exhaustively in Annie Hill's fantastic book. *Voyaging on a Small Income*. Although the figures are a little out of date, it is still a very inspirational book for budget sailors and full of great advice.

On no account buy your boat with debt. If you do this, you will simply import the stresses from land onto the sea. Don't even buy a boat that is expensive to maintain, park or lift (i.e., a large boat or any size catamaran), even if you have the purchase price in cash. Large boats mean big bills, which in turn means you will be back in the same old routine of constantly obsessing about money and wondering why you ever left the shore.

Do not bring land snobbery to the sea. If you are the type who always needs to have the flashiest car or the biggest house, then you may to have to change your attitude to become a happy sea gypsy (see chapter 3 Getting Real). I knew a couple in Australia who had sold their house and spent the money on a $600,000 catamaran. They never seemed to go anywhere or even leave the boat. On closer questioning, I discovered that they only got $400,000 for the house and borrowed the rest! For a sea gypsy, this is madness. For less than $50,000, they could have bought a conservative little sea boat with enough cash left to generate an income and set sail without a care in the world. Read that again: Without a care in the world!

With a little change of attitude they could be seeing the most beautiful spots on the planet, making some new friends of all different shapes and colours, learning their sea-craft and generally living the dream. Instead, they are in the same tiny marina in Australia whining about how expensive boating is while what remains of their youth withers on the vine.

Do you really want to put yourself through this? Would it not be better and cheaper to stick a pin in the ego and start breathing again?

Small boats are waaaaayy cooler anyway! Recently, while we were anchored in lovely Nuku Hiva in the Marquesas, a beautiful little pea-green, gaff-rigged cutter sailed into the bay and all heads turned to look at her as she glided in under full main and tops'l gallant. Resentment was the only feeling we had towards the ostentatious million dollar motor-sailor that was blocking our view of her.

I realise what I am asking here is a complete change in values for many people. But for most, it is just a question of a slight change of perspective - and most people are quite capable of doing this. Surely it cannot be too difficult to see what a privilege it is to explore this beautiful watery world from the deck of your own small windship without worrying about whether somebody else has a more expensive one? (Someone always does!)

Do not be fooled into buying loads of unnecessary gear. Remember, that whatever you buy will need to be fitted, which can often be another 50% of the purchase price. (With our new fuel tanks, it was 300% of the purchase price!). Just about everything you add to your boat will need maintaining much more often than a similar item on land and maintenance costs know no upper limit. Perhaps when you have settled into your new life and established yourself, there will be money for toys. For now, stick to the essentials.

So, now you have your modest little sea boat, which you have put into good sea-worthy condition. You have chosen well, so your outgoings are low. You have learnt heaps and saved a fortune by avoiding marine professionals and doing most of the work yourself. Are you now sustainable? If you don't have a little nest egg generating income, then the answer is probably 'No'. The good news is that having chosen well, stuck a pin in your ego and kept your expenses low, it will be relatively easy to become sustainable as a little income goes a long way on a sea gypsy boat!

The money that Jasna and I live on comes largely from writing with a little interest on our savings bringing up the rear. We have no debts and no dependents. Time for us is just time. In fact, stopping in Bora Bora for weeks on end, far from costing the Earth (as it would if you were still making payments on your boat, car or house) can actually increase our gypsy funds. When we are anchored somewhere nice for a while we:

- Have more time to earn a living.

- Are not using *Calypso* and therefore reducing wear and tear.

- Can shop around for the cheapest supplies (usually direct from farms).

- Trade our skills for supplies. (There is some good footage of us doing this on Ben Fogle's *New Lives in the Wild*. Series 4, Episode 4).

Now, not everybody has the skills or desire to put in the amount of computer time it takes to compete in the increasingly competitive world of travel journalism, but there are a million other ways to earn as you go. Below are just a few suggestions. REMEMBER: Because you have gotten real and reduced your overheads as far as possible by adopting the sea gypsy approach, you only need to earn a small amount to live well. You will not need to kill yourself struggling to pay the whopping bills generated by flashy, large, overcomplicated boats. A marine mechanic can earn in a few days, what we spend in a month, so let's start there.

Marine Mechanic. Diesels and Outboards. If you are a decent mechanic, get some cards printed, oil your tools and away you go. I can't tell you how much the marine world needs good mechanics. If you are presentable, punctual and do not have severe attitude problems, you will be a rare commodity indeed.

Marine Canvas: If you can use a sewing machine, then you can make a good living making sail covers, biminis, outboard and dinghy covers, spray hoods etc. If you can't use a sewing machine, but fancy this line of work, take an evening class. It is not a difficult skill to acquire. A friend of ours on the sister ship to *Calypso* did exactly this and was so overwhelmed with work, that she kept upping her prices. When this failed to deter her clients, she packed it in all together for the peace and quiet.

Sail Repair: This takes a little longer to learn and requires a more expensive machine, but may suit someone who is already interested in the subject. Definitely pays well though.

Marine refrigeration. Another thing you can learn at evening class and does not require too many specialised large tools. We have a very good friend who does this. He is very reasonably priced for fellow sea gypsies, but when the big yacht pulls in, he shaves, sprays his armpits (probably with WD40), puts on his spotless white overalls and pops over with his business card. Marine refrigeration (along with marine water-makers) are fantastically unreliable which is a pain in the butt if you own one, an enormous pain if you own an enormous one, but a regular pay day for the Fridge Guy.

Cooking. If you can produce decent lasagne, pizza, cookies, etc, at a good price, you can take orders and deliver when you are in a popular anchorage. Quite few people do this and it is a great way to get to know your new neighbours – there is even a French Pastry Guy in Barra de Navidad on the Mexican west coast who would bang on our hull at about 6am with all kinds of yummy stuff. To date, this was the only period in our lives where Jasna was consistently out of bed before me.

Affiliate Programmes If you don't know what these are, there is a great book about how to use affiliate programmes called *Living a Laptop Lifestyle.* You can buy it through our website www.sailingcalypso.com.

If you just bought it, great! You just got a fantastic book and we just made two dollars. Now do you get what affiliate programmes do?

Amazon was the first company to start an affiliate programme, but now thousands of companies have them and you can earn money by recommending their products. In our opinion there is an unspoken code of honour operating here. If you are prepared to recommend anything at all to earn a buck, then you have kind of missed the point of the sea gypsy ethos and simply become a salesman. Stick to recommending only those things that you have an extremely positive personal experience of and then there is no need to 'sell' anything. For example, we recommend Cape Horn wind vanes. Do we get a commission when you buy one? Well in this case, we do not, but it would make no difference if we did. We recommend Cape Horn wind vanes because we use one in the big testing tank and it has wildly exceeded our expectations and steers our boat like Captain Cook on ice skates. We do not need to lie or 'sell' the things we recommend because we only recommend the stuff we use and love and would recommend anyway. Sometimes that pays a commission, sometimes it doesn't. If you are out to make as much money as you can without consciousness, you may be happier ashore with the other sharks. (NOTE: all sailors know that most sharks live on land).

Chartering: We have many friends who do this and make a decent living. However, because it costs so much to buy and licence a charter boat, it is not really within the scope of this book, which is more aimed at those without such resources. Nevertheless, if you have ignored all the advice in this book and gone boat shopping as if you were looking for an apartment, saddled yourself with a massively expensive catamaran and no income, then this might be the only way to redeem yourself. Remember though that you will need to qualify as a skipper and get the boat licensed for charter – all of which cost money.

Black (unlicensed) Charter: We do not recommend this and do not do it ourselves. However, there are plenty of people out there who stop somewhere for a while (the San Blas islands near Panama have been in vogue recently) and charter their boat and crew to the public. We choose not to do this because although nobody ever seems to get prosecuted, it is, strictly speaking, illegal – and looking over our shoulder is not part of our philosophy. However, each situation and country is different and that is for you to assess and decide. There is certainly some money to be made.

Having Guests. Now this is a whole different biscuit of weevils and something we do often. A charter is where a person or persons pay you a fee to use your boat and crew for an agreed purpose. A pretty good fee too! We have nothing to do with that.

What we do on board *Calypso* is offer people the chance to join us as volunteer crew (i.e., they have to work). They come with us wherever we are going (we do not make any special arrangements or detours, nor does the visitor have the right to suggest any). We make no charge for this, but all volunteers must pay a daily fee towards food and the general expenses of running a boat. You will not see a cash profit like this (if you do, then good, put it aside for the next time somebody loses your dinghy paddle or puts their butt through your spray hood), but it is great for making new friends, keeping the stainless steel shiny and helping with the expenses.

Diver: Can you dive? Do you have your own gear? There is plenty of work for divers doing various jobs below the waterline on boats. Not even rich boats haul out just to change their anodes or clean their propeller. This is a very good way to earn a few gypsy tokens for those who love diving and my idea of hell on stilts (well, we can't all be the same).

Rigger: If you have an engineering background and a head for heights, this is a skill that can be acquired fairly quickly as it is simple structural engineering. This is particularly true with today's swage-less compression fittings, which are easily assembled without the need for huge hydraulic presses. I am not suggesting you get up there and 'wing it', but if your dream is to be a sea gypsy and drop out of the rat race for good, this would be a great, portable skill to have. Remember, if you see a problem that is out of your depth, you can always refer it to a more experienced rigger and make a friend. Next time he is too busy to do a job, maybe he will recommend you. He may even employ you to assist and you can learn how to fix it yourself next time you are asked.

You will also get quite fit, super-tanned and find strange women looking at you for a fraction of a second longer than strictly appropriate.

Paid Newsletter. Jasna publishes a weekly newsletter by subscription only. The newsletter costs 20 Euros a year and is full of photos, tips on living the gypsy life and stories from around the world. One subscriber called it "a little ray of sunshine in my inbox". (If you want to subscribe, drop us an email). Once you get going, you could do the same. Why wait until you get going? Why not blog your adventure of *becoming* a sea gypsy? If you do, send us the link – sounds like a great story!

Web Designer. All over the world there are businesses who have heard of the power of the internet but who think a server is someone who brings you a drink. With a little experience and a budget hosting/domain name plan in your back pocket, you can put them in touch with the world and make a living too.

Musician. Nah. Just kidding. Not a chance. Do you know the difference between a musician and a large pizza? A large pizza can feed a family of four.

These are just the obvious ones. Your imagination is the limit (especially with e-commerce ramping up). We once met a troop on board a French boat who were all acrobats. They would set up a trapeze between the masts of their enormous ketch and put on an amazing circus show in marinas and anchorages. Best $10 I ever spent!

How sea gypsies make their living is just as varied as those onshore, but with the advantage that our expenses are much lower, our desires fulfilled by nature and our minds so mercifully free from the ravages of land-based values, that we don't feel the need to kill ourselves to climb the greasy pole of ambition or amass more than we need.

Flexibility is the key though, and this is another good reason to be debt-free and not to fixate about going around the world or getting some more miles under the keel.
For example, if you arrive in Sydney and get offered a good rigging contract for the next three months, you need to be able to take it, as this would set you up for the year. If you have to refuse the job because you have to get back home to work in order to pay off your whopping mortgage, or you have fixated upon 'achieving' more distance this year, then you will have to pass. Time and money get all mixed up again as every missed opportunity bleeds the life out of your bank account. Every day that goes by you get poorer and poorer and this puts the same financial strain on your sailing life as you had in your land life.

Jasna and I are now totally sustainable. We didn't start that way, but we have kept at it and now even put a little aside each month. We do all this whilst sailing around beautiful islands, meeting new people and old friends, and drinking home-made wine and coconut rum with them. All around the world there are hundreds of sea gypsies doing the same.

Some are carpenters, some play the stock market. Some fix engines, others paint boats. Some do black charter and others have an internet business; but they all live an idyllic life aboard their affordable, small sea-boats. You can too.

Part Two
Staying Real

Introduction to Part Two

Unless you live in an active volcano, there are few environments on Earth more corrosive or unpredictable than warm, salt water. This can be challenging sometimes. For the owner of the wrong boat, it can often be overwhelming.

Even with a simple, wholesome sea-boat of the type described in this book, every sailor will have to develop some skill in creative problem solving. With the right boat though, you will be able to embrace this challenge and learn from it. Like many watery wanderers, Jasna and I enjoy the challenge of creative problem solving and derive a great deal of pleasure from finding simple solutions for the common questions that are posed by *Calypso* as she makes her way around the saltier parts of the planet. It may seem a little overwhelming at first, but you will soon start to enjoy it.

However, if all your problems can be traced back to the fact that you bought a badly designed boat that is full of unnecessary and vulnerable toys, costs a fortune to operate and sails like a log cabin with a stick in it, then every time things are going badly, you will be reminded of this. Every time you get into a bit of bad weather and your in-mast furling jams, you will be kicking yourself. Every time your massive aft cabin causes your boat to steer like a wilful pig, you will be reminded of your foolishness. Every time you are asked to pay an outrageous bill for your enormous boat, you will be hurled back into the same arena of financial anxiety that you had hoped was finally behind you.

Part One of this book was designed to help you avoid some of the more common mistakes that inevitably lead to this type of dissatisfaction with the sailing life. Once you have got your mind in the right shape and bought the right boat, your problems will be righteous problems – invitations to learn, rather than a telegram reminding you of what a sucker you have been with a gilt-edged offer to join the wonderful world of consumer yachting attached to it.

Even if you have ignored every bit of advice in Part One, there are still some tips and philosophies in Part Two that might help you, but in the end you can't polish a turd - even a shiny, expensive one with a dishwasher and microwave. If however, you have taken on board what we are saying and can see the logic in it, then Part Two will be the icing on the cake.

We are still out there making mistakes, solving problems, getting better at what we do and there is still much to learn. Part Two is a selection of some of the more important things we have learnt as we become better sea gypsies. It is by no means exhaustive, but we hope that what we have learnt solving our problems helps you enjoy solving yours.
We welcome all comments and insights on creative problem solving on our website: www.sailingcalypso.com.

Chapter 11

Staying Put – The Importance of Good Anchors

As discussed, marinas are perhaps the number one item on the sea gypsy's 'avoid' list along with customs officials, import duty and STDs. The cost of a marina alone is more than our entire monthly budget. What's more, they are crowded, noisy and some have rats or cockroaches that can run up your dock lines and up your shorts. Marinas are a total waste of money. Yet many people flock to them - sometimes because they are living elsewhere and only visiting their boat at the odd weekend, but many because they have never learned to be comfortable at anchor.

We attended a meeting of 'Puddle Jumpers' (a rather optimistically dismissive term for people who are intending to cross the Pacific) in Puerto Vallarta a few years ago. About half of those who were crossing were on fairly new production boats and had never anchored before (one boat still had the price tag attached to her shiny new anchor). It is a source of amazement to me that many boats that have fancy electronics, water makers, microwaves, water carbonators, freezers, electric winches etc., do not have decent anchors or know how to use them well.

When one of the big yacht rallies comes through the anchorage you are staying in, keep a weather eye open. Just a week ago on the island of Tahuata, in our favourite anchorage, the Blue Planet rally all showed up at once in their enormous, flashy yachts, dropped their anchors in a most perfunctory way and before the silt had settled, were already in their over-powered ribs scattering turtles on their quest to be the first ashore.

Not surprisingly, three of them dragged out to sea in the night and it was dumb luck that no other boats were damaged. I am sure they have mountains of insurance which allows them to be more blasé than we poor sea gypsies, but insured or not, serious damage to your hull will take time and trouble to fix even if it is not your fault, so you need to learn about your ground tackle and watch out for those who haven't learnt about theirs.

As you have guessed by now, this book focuses mainly on creating the right attitude, rather than on every technical detail of sailing, but this chapter is going to be a bit of an exception. This is because you can take all the time you want to learn the finer points of sail trimming, engine servicing, sail repair, yacht cuisine and on which side of boat a polite person is expected to puke over (downwind) while you become accustomed to your new life in the nice sunny place you have chosen. Anchoring is about the only skill you need to get right from the very beginning, so in a complete departure from style, we are going to get instructional. Firstly though, a word on depth sounders.

A Word About Depth Sounders

There is no doubt that the depth sounder is an important bit of gear on a boat. It is one of the few bits of electronic equipment that I would not like to live without. Depth sounders are fairly reliable and useful. Nowhere is this more obvious than when

---

anchoring.

But beware! Most depth sounders are fitted on the hull, beside the keel and need to be set up with an 'offset' in order to read the depth of water *under* the keel. They are all different, but check the operator's manual (don't worry if you did not inherit a manual with the boat as most of them are online these days) and make sure this is the figure you are seeing on the display or remember to make allowances for the depth of the keel in your calculations if it is not.

Anchors 101

There are many different types of anchor, all of which have their fans. The main criteria for your principal anchor is that it must be of the ploughing or scooping type, correctly sized on the right chain and swivel. You will need at least 50 meters of chain with another 50 meters of good rope spliced on the end. Once you have all that, you will need it all again for the second anchor (although many sailors have a little more rope than chain on the second anchor to save weight). This is the minimum requirement. Ideally, you would also have a smaller stern anchor with 10 meters of chain and 30 meters of rope, and a collapsible, over-sized storm anchor in the bilge.

We have a Delta anchor and a Bruce on the front of the boat and an aluminium Fortress as a stern anchor. We don't currently have a storm anchor, but it is on our radar. You will also need good chain and it is unlikely that the previous owner of your boat bought new chain once he started thinking about selling. If you are in a fairly developed country, it will be possible to have your existing chain tested and re-galvanized, but seeing as you have no idea whether it was decent chain to begin with, it pays to sell it at the next boat jumble or to a local fisherman and put the money towards some new, quality (i.e., not Chinese) chain. Even so, when you get your new chain, check every link. We would have lost our boat if Jasna had not spotted an open link on our brand new chain from a reputed American manufacturer. To get our refund we were required to sign a silence clause, so we can't name and shame them! Now, once you have got all this stuff, you need to learn how to use it.

Technique

The magic word in anchoring is 'scope'. This describes the amount of chain or rope (or mixture of both) you have out compared to the depth. Having enough scope is essential to good anchoring. Five times the depth is good, seven times the depth is better and ten times the depth is fantastic (though rarely practical).

Choosing a spot to anchor is often a compromise. If you are the only boat in a wide bay with good holding sand, then the world is your lobster. However, there will often be obstacles and other boats. Generally you are looking to be in the windward end of the anchorage over good holding sand and clear of any other boats or obstructions. Always try and imagine where your boat will be if the wind changes direction and/or when the tide reverses, and if you get a voice in your head that says 'on the beach' then now might be a good time to anchor further out. Getting figures for tidal flow is very easy these days, you don't even have to be online. I have figures for everywhere in the world downloaded on my computer, so there are no excuses to fall foul of an ebbing tide.

There are complicated methods to work out the tides to the last centimeter and you will have to demonstrate a knowledge of these if you want to become a qualified skipper, but basically look at the difference between high an low tide (the tidal range) and make sure you are anchored in several feet more than that, and all will be well. For example, if the tidal range is 6 feet and you have 14 feet under your keel, then it does not really matter too much which phase the tide is in (it is good seamanship to know, but this is a good rule of thumb if you are pressed for time). If the tidal range is 6 feet and you can only put six feet of water under your keel, then it becomes vital that you know which phase the tide is in. If it is low tide, then no worries, if it is nearer high tide then you could be in for a nasty grounding. (I got this catastrophically wrong in Australia opposite the Royal Yachting Association office where I had recently qualified as a Skipper. Very embarrassing indeed).

Always err on the side of caution and never fixate on trying to reproduce that tourist brochure image of a boat 6 feet off the beach with the happy nuclear family swimming ashore to pick bananas. The minute the photographer got that shot, the skipper would have probably anchored further out anyway.

Also be aware that catamarans often swing the other way when the wind changes (particularly in tidal flows) and try and anchor with other monohulls (the owners are much more likely to be fellow sea gypsies anyway).

Approach your chosen anchor spot directly into the wind if you are on engine power or as close as you can if under sail. Bring your boat to a stop (turn dead into the wind if under sail) and drop the anchor so that it just touches the sea bed. For example, if your depth sounder is reading 10 meters, drop just enough chain (probably 13 meters to account for the distance between the bow and the bottom of the keel. See above for more info on depth sounders).

Using the wind (or the engine in dead slow reverse) allow the boat to move *slowly* backwards as you *slowly* let out more chain. The idea is to match the speed you drop the chain with the backward motion of the boat so you lay out the chain in a nice straight line. If your partner is going too fast backwards, then lay out the chain a little more quickly or ask her to slow down by reducing or cutting the power to the engine or easing the sheets (if under sail).

The idea is to lay out the chain in a straight line rather than dump a big pile of it on top of the anchor. Imagine you are decorating a cake; you need to start moving at the same moment (or slightly before) as you start squeezing the icing bag, or you end up with a big blob of icing at the beginning. Once you have paid out at least 5 times the depth (in this case 50m) use a nylon line with a chain hook (see picture) or a rolling hitch to take the strain off the windlass gypsy (anchor winch) so you can test your anchor. Attach the line to a solid deck fitting so that all the strain from the anchor chain is being directed there. This line will later become your snubber (see below).

Testing (the forgotten step!)

Slip the boat into slow reverse and *gently* take the strain on your chain. You will feel and see the bow of the boat swing around as the chain comes under tension. Keep the strain on and slowly increase the revs of the engine. I like to increase the revs in increments of about 20% and give each setting 20 seconds or so to allow the anchor to really dig in. Do this until you are at full power (or as close as you can get without stressing the engine) and check you are not moving.

NOTE: We use full power because we have a small engine. If your boat has a powerful engine, you will need to use less. Gradually shut the power down. If you shut the power down all in one go, the weight of the chain falling to the sea bed will pull the boat forward and the momentum will undo all your earlier good work as the chain doubles back on itself and possibly wraps around something.

Congratulations, you are now anchored more securely than most boats! In clear waters you can also get your mask on and check your anchor visually, but that is not always possible. Don't worry too much –if you have followed the above steps and tested the anchor well, you can relax. NOTE: Anchoring in coral is a bit more complicated and is covered on our website.

Adding a Snubber

In strong winds your boat will try and move away from the anchor and that will transfer some snatch loading onto the windlass. A snubber is a length of rope you attach to the chain that can stretch and absorb some of this load. In reality, the great length of heavy chain being lifted off the sea bed as your boat moves away from its anchor absorbs much of the loading, but the snubber is useful for other purposes too. Firstly it allows you to divert the load of the chain from your expensive windlass (which could be easily damaged by the constant snatching of a gusty anchorage), onto a solid deck fitting; and secondly, it helps protect your hull from being scratched by the chain. We use a chain hook to attach our snubber to the chain, but you could just as easily tie a rolling hitch or use a shackle.

If, like us, you have a bowsprit and a bobstay, a snubber led through a snatch block at the end of the bowsprit will give you a much quieter night than allowing the snubber to chafe away at the bobstay (please note that this technique is only suitable for relatively calm anchorages as it transfers much of the load from the anchor up the forestay to the mast. In rough anchorages, bring your snubber more inboard and check regularly for chafing). There are many ways to set snubbers and one will be right for your boat - see your fellow sea gypsies for tips and find what works for you, but always bear in mind where you will be transferring the snatching loads.

Riding Sails

Some boats sit nicely at anchor, but many will sail around to a certain extent in gusty winds. This can increase snatch loads and can even dislodge your anchor. It also scares the life out of other boats in the anchorage. We saw one catamaran in Mexico that danced around so violently, it was hard not to believe it possessed by the ghost of Montezuma.

Fortunately, there is a very simple solution to this, which has largely been forgotten and is rarely seen these days - the riding sail. Basically, this is a small sail that you run up the backstay or the topping lift that makes your boat `weathercock` into the wind. A riding sail can be an old dinghy sail or can be custom made quite cheaply and will keep your boat pointed into the wind, reduce snatching and chafe to virtually nothing and seriously reduce the use of valium in the anchorage. We have one on *Calypso* and use it often.

Setting a Second Anchor

In extreme conditions, you might want to add a second anchor for a bit of extra security. There are basically two ways of doing this. If you have advanced notice of a deterioration in conditions, it makes sense to attach a second anchor with its own swivel to the existing chain a few meters behind the first anchor. (A swivel is an attachment that allows the chain to turn without turning the anchor. You probably already have one with the boat you inherited, if so, get another, if not, get two). This system works well because the main reason boats drag is poor grip on the sea bed (rather than chains breaking which is extremely rare).

If you get caught short by an unpredicted change in the weather, you may not be able to safely raise the anchor and add another behind it. In this case, motor forward at about 50 degrees to your first anchor (reeling in a little slack on the original rode if necessary) and drop the second on its own dedicated chain and then reverse back, using the same technique as above (remember the icing bag?). This is much easier to do in a pinch than attaching a second anchor to the existing chain and you have the added security of never being detached from the sea bed. Be careful not to tangle your original rode in your propeller whilst performing this operation or you will be in a right pickle.

However, with two separate rodes, there is always the risk that they can tangle if the boat swings, and that can make retrieval difficult. This may be your only choice though if you are caught out and leaving the anchorage is not an option.
You can reduce the risk of tangling by keeping a good angle

between the rodes – the closer they are together, the higher the likelihood of a snarl up – and bringing one in before the wind dies completely or changes direction and you start to swing.

You can reduce the risk of losing your anchor by attaching a float or fender to it (before you drop it, duh!) with a line slightly longer than the depth at high tide. Then, if you have to ditch the anchor for any reason, you can find it again later. Attach the line to the front of the anchor (many anchors have a hole for this purpose) and it will also act as a 'trip' and make retrieval easier should the anchor become stuck. Attaching a float also has the added advantage of signaling the position of your anchor to other sailors who might otherwise be tempted to politely drop an anchor of their own on top of it.

Stern Anchoring

Unless an anchorage is so crowded or small that it is dangerous to allow your boat to swing, stern anchoring is used more for comfort than safety. In many anchorages, the swell comes from a different direction than the wind. As a boat at anchor usually faces into the wind or tide, this can mean that your floating home is sideways to the swell and rolling about like a drunk on a snowboard. This can be quite uncomfortable for long periods and can actually start to affect your sense of humour after a while. While I would never bother setting a stern anchor for a night or two, if you are staying put for a while, it will pay off.

The easiest way to set a stern anchor is to wait until there is little wind or that the wind and swell are temporarily working together and your boat is facing into the swell (this can happen quite often in an anchorage with a mountainous backdrop, as the wind tends to whip around a bit or diminish to the point that the tide is determining which way you are facing). What Jasna and I do is we anchor normally and roll around like drunks for a while. As soon as the rolling stops, this is our signal that we are facing into the swell and it will now be easy to set the stern anchor. We start the fiery stinkbox (engine) and slowly reverse whilst letting out our entire 100 meters of anchor rode. We then chuck the stern anchor over the back (having first attached a fender to it to warn other sailors that we are stern anchored) and slowly pull half the bow rode in with the windlass whilst letting out an equal amount of rode at the stern until we are suspended between the two anchors facing the swell with a clearly marked stern anchor. Voila! [9]

If the wind is more constant, it is unlikely that your boat will ever find herself naturally facing into the swell, so you will have to use your dinghy. Drop the anchor and rode into the dinghy and pay out the rode as you find the spot that will haul your stern around and point your bow into the swell. Drop the anchor over the side of the dinghy and then the onboard crew can slowly haul the stern around until you are properly aligned. This method is much more hassle. Also the rusty

---

[9] One sailor I know drops his stern anchor out first and motors forward into the swell until all the rode is paid out and the anchor bites. He then drops the bow anchor and drifts back, slowly letting the bow rode out while simultaneously pulling in the stern rode. This technique has the advantage of being workable whatever the wind is doing because boats can better choose their direction going forward pulling against a stern anchor, than going backwards pulling against a bow anchor. I have never tried this technique because like many other boats, I simply don't carry enough stern rode to end up with a decent amount out once the bow anchor is set. Sounds cool though.

chain, locking wire and shackles on the anchor can seriously damage an inflatable dinghy (yet another reason not to have one), but this is what you will have to do if the wind and swell are not cooperating. It is advisable to get fairly proficient at this in an uncrowded anchorage, as in some places there is no alternative.

Hiva Oa in the Marquesas is the first stop for many people crossing the Pacific and the little harbour of Atuona is so crowded in April that all boats are stern anchored facing the sea like spawning salmon contemplating a waterfall. If you drag your stern anchor in this situation, you will wipe out a lot of boats, so don't be doing it for the first time in a harbour like this. The key is, as always, to practice in benign conditions so that you know what you are doing when the going gets tougher or when there is more at stake.

Anchoring Etiquette

Always give your fellow sailors plenty of room. If you think you are too close, you probably are. If a sailor comes and expresses his concerns, it is up to you to move. Do not get defensive and stubborn. If you stay put, not only will you create tension in paradise, but if you later swing into anyone who was already anchored before you showed up, you will be liable for the damages. Fortunately, the only time I have had any lip from people who have anchored too close has been from organized rally participants. In this case, simply contact the rally leader who will understand the rules a little better than the wealthy dilettantes in his charge, and insist the offending boat moves. On the rare occasions I am forced to anchor anywhere that is a little tight, I drop my kayak in the water and paddle over to my closest neighbour and ask;

'Do you think I am a little close?'

Usually the action of asking creates a good feeling and assures the skipper that you are not the kind of mindless playboy who doesn't realise he might be a little close or possibly doesn't care because his boat is bigger than yours and better insured. If you are making someone uncomfortable, always move and always do it with a smile.

Anchoring Communication

We generally see more bad communication anchoring than anywhere else and bad communication leads to accidents and disagreements. The anchor winch is a heavy industrial machine carrying industrial strength loads and should be treated with the same sort of respect as a band saw. The bigger the boat, the bigger the loads and the bigger the danger. Unfortunately, bigger boats also increase the chances of communication break down as couples try and shout along greater distances and subsequently vent their frustrations when their commands are misunderstood. Here are some tips on using it without injury to body or spirit.

Establish who is the boss.

A boat is not a democracy and it is neither desirable nor practical for every decision to go to committee. There will be a skipper and her word will be law. On *Calypso* we share the skipper's responsibilities, but for each task, one of us will be the boss. The important thing is not to have two bosses for the same task. For anchoring, it is very much Jasna's time to be skipper. Jasna likes to drop the anchor, which means that it is her hands in the machinery. This automatically means that she is the boss. Whatever task you are doing on a boat, the one with their body at risk calls the shots. Whilst Jasna is anchoring, I am at the helm and it would be madness for me to start making unilateral decisions, like when to motor forward or backwards, while she has her hands in the chain. This way doth lie grievous injury and divorce.

Establish a good system of communication.

We use hand signals that we have invented ourselves to cover all the commands needed to anchor. Invent your own - it's fun! Hand signals are best because they have a clear meaning and they avoid the need to shout. You may only be shouting to be heard above the wind, but your partner may not see it that way, particularly if a little stress creeps into your voice, so it is good to avoid shouting altogether. On the rare occasions where Jasna needs to give a more complicated instruction, she walks halfway down the deck and speaks in a near-normal voice. To make sure she knows I have heard and understood her, I repeat the command. For example, if she makes a hand signal, I make the same one in reply. If she says,

"Go around again because the sea bed is too rocky here", I will immediately repeat the essence of the command. I will say,

"Going around again" and get on with it.

If you do not establish a hierarchy for this (or every other) task and a good communication system to implement it, somebody is going to get hurt. At the very least you will be sleeping on the couch.

Never touch the chain with your hands.

We have a stainless steel pole attached by a string that is permanently with the windlass. If there is a jam or something untoward, we do not try and fix that jam by hand. Rather, we use the stick. This means that should the chain suddenly spin out, we will not spend the rest of our lives needing both hands to order five beers and resenting our partner because he can play the piano. If the problem is too complicated to be fixed with a stick (unlikely), then lock off the windlass, take the weight of the chain and anchor with a snubber and lash it off to a strong point. Only then go near it with your hands. If you have a powered windlass, shut the power off too in case some dufus sits on the control or accidentally stands on the footswitch while you are playing cat's cradle with the chain.

Good! Now you and your main squeeze can anchor safely and well. You also stand a much better chance of staying together. But before we bring this rather technical chapter to a close, a word about swinging at anchor.

If you are anchored in a nice wee bay with a constant wind blowing, it is unlikely that you will swing. However, if the wind changes you will swing to face the new direction. Even if the wind only drops out, you will probably still swing with the tide. When this happens, your anchor will either totally or partially pop up from the seabed and then re-dig itself in again. You are quite vulnerable at this point to dragging, so if you are in a very strong tidal anchorage, it pays to stay onboard until after the first change in tide to make sure your anchor is digging in again nicely. If you have a stern anchor out, you will not swing of course, but watch out for those boats that will – that million dollar catamaran might have looked far away on the incoming tide, but it will be an awful lot closer when it swings around its 50 meters of rode when the tide changes!

The important thing is to have an anchor that buries itself quickly and efficiently and pretty much the worst performer in this category, both in my opinion and that of *YACHTING* magazine's test department, is the CQR[10]. The CQR is a kind of plough anchor with a head that pivots. I mention this because these are what you find on many older boats and I don't trust them further than I can spit a winch handle. There are some fabulous anchors on the market now: The Delta (a very economical and effective anchor from Lewmar), the Rocna, the Spade, the Bruce (great once it is in, but difficult to set if there are any weeds).

If you inherit a CQR with your boat, sell it at the next boat jumble and put the money towards some decent anchors. This is NOT an area in which you can be budget conscious. I know, I know.... good anchors are expensive and I feel your pain my gypsy brothers and sisters, but do not try and economise here and do not buy Chinese knock-off. Remember, a good Delta

---

[10] To be fair, the Danforth and the Fisherman anchors are the worst, but hardly anybody uses a Danforth as a bow anchor and the fisherman anchor is only really for rock and weed, so it is not a fair comparison.

anchor costs less than a month in a marina and will last forever.

When the wind pipes up and your oversized Delta is clutching you to the seabed like a nervous clam with abandonment issues, you will be very happy you bought decent ground tackle and took the time to learn to use it properly. When your expensive neighbours are dragging out to sea and you are feeling righteously smug, don't forget to say to yourself, "I must buy those *Calypso* guys a beer when we cross watery paths". (Oh, go on then, just the one).

Chapter 12

The Fiery Stinkbox – Engines 101

Internal combustion engines are very much a mixed blessing on a sailing boat. They add a lot of weight, expense, increase the risk of fire, produce greenhouse gasses and need vigilant maintenance. I admire very much those sailors whose engine-less vessels take to the waters without the noxious diesel engine spoiling the ambience. These are the elite sailors in my opinion and I completely understand the allure of sailing without the fiery stinkbox. (I once had to bring a 45 foot sloop into a crowded marina under sail after the propeller had dropped off. I still remember the rush of satisfaction it gave me as her enormous hull glided softly up to the pontoon as the sails simultaneously clattered into the jacks – right in front of the Sunday lunch crowd. It almost made me wish I smoked a pipe).

Several times I have stood on an engine-less boat and admired the systems the owners have in place for efficient sail handling and manoeuvring under sail alone. Yet standing on the deck of a boat such as this does not make you a great sailor any more than standing in a hospital makes you a neurosurgeon. These guys have honed their craft and their skills to the point where this is a safe and rewarding way for them to sail. For the budding sea gypsy (and it pains me to say it) some sort of engine is essential, at least for your first boat. There are two very good reasons for this.

1. Safety

It is undeniably true that many great sailors have circumnavigated and even mapped the world under sail alone. What is important to remember is that for every *Endeavour*, there are literally dozens of shipwrecked boats that were battered against rocks when the wind changed and they found themselves at the mercy of the current when close to shore. Modern boats can beat off a lee shore in strong winds, but even modern boats are powerless to prevent being taken by the current when the wind suddenly dies completely without some sort of engine. Perhaps the most famous engine-less sea gypsy boat of all time, *Erik the Red,* was lost in this rather ignominious manner in fairly benign conditions.

For a novice crew, safety can also be compromised by the panic that comes from inexperience. Say for example, you are anchored in a nice little bay, but during the night the wind changes and you find yourself in a bubbling cauldron, being pushed onto the beach. The novice sailor without an engine is going to find it quite stressful to get the anchor up and beat out of a small bay because to do it right, much will depend on extremely accurate helming, spot-on sail trimming and good judgment. Is the new sailor really expected to do this in the dark and to do it calmly without errors? Much more likely he will move too quickly in all directions at once, trip over something and end up face-planting the bilge whilst his pride and joy makes friends with the beach.

The engine-less novice, faced with this problem may even elect to stay and ride it out – putting himself at greater risk than the other sailors who have started up the fiery stinkbox and high-tailed it over to the protected side of the island. At the very least, the stress caused by constantly worrying about having to do this is enough to warrant the inclusion of an engine in a sailboat.

There is a school of thought that says you should always be ready to beat out of a bay using your sails alone for those times when your engine fails, and that the engine-less boat owner, having become accustomed to doing this is inherently safer.

This is nonsense on stilts.

It is quite easy to have your cake and eat it by doing what Jasna and I do. We start the engine and leave it in neutral. We then try and get out of the problem under sail alone. Normally we get this right. If not, we slip the nicely warmed up engine into forward and thank our lucky stars for it and all the dead dinosaurs that make it work. At a more convenient moment we will try and work out what we did wrong and thus gain experience without risking our boat or our bacon.

2. Exploring

Not having some means of mechanical propulsion aboard will also limit the places you can cruise. Many harbours are fantastically well protected against wind and you will need to avoid many of them in anything less than ideal conditions. Should you be brave enough to enter under sail alone, you could soon find yourself with slack sails and drifting with the current the moment you are in the lee of a massive cliff. Furthermore, these protected anchorages are often strafed by katabatic winds (sudden gusts of cool air rushing down a mountain) which are going to knock you flat on your arse, or blow out your sails as you spread every bit of canvas in order to capture what little wind there is.

Many of the best storm hideouts are often at the head of long, narrow channels or mangrove swamps that are only accessible by powered boats. It would be a shame to be so near a good refuge and not be able to access it.

I could go on forever about the advantages of having some kind of engine, but I fear that may give the wrong impression. We would be the first to throw the engine overboard if we considered it safe because, like so many others at sea, we are acutely aware of our environmental impact. They are also expensive, complicated and noisy. I certainly do not recommend that you become part of the growing tendency to have ridiculously over-sized engines and use them practically all the time. There are lots of middle ways. Here are some examples from current sea gypsies.

1. Rick and Jasna on *Calypso*

Our middle way is possibly the easiest to follow as the boat you buy will probably already have some kind of diesel engine, or at least be set up to take one. We have a small tractor engine made by the UK company *Perkins*. We order all our spares from agricultural outlets, therefore avoiding marine suppliers. It is a simple engine, which means we can do all the work on her ourselves and we only use her when absolutely necessary (and never to charge the batteries - see chapter 14). We behave as if we don't own an engine at all. Most years we burn about 150 litres of fuel which means we run our engine about 90 hours a year. We sail everywhere and use our engine responsibly (we do not run the engine flat out as this drives the fuel consumption through the roof just for the sake of another knot or two). If there is no wind, we wait until there is. Relax, enjoy the anchorage, or if you are at sea, spread your biggest light wind sail and enjoy the beauty of sailing slowly on a calm ocean. That's why we are here is it not? Still, our engine has saved our bacon several times and although we use it sparingly, it is nice to know it is there.

2. Captain Dan on *Misty*

When Captain Dan built his diminutive 26ft cutter *Misty* he decided to bypass the whole diesel engine installation entirely and fit a bracket on the stern that allows him to drop a 5hp long shaft outboard into the water to power him the last half a mile or so into an anchorage. Dan is a proper sea gypsy, so that is all he needs. There are certain advantages to the outboard idea:

Cost

A small outboard is much cheaper than a marine diesel. Furthermore, outboards are much easier to replace than diesel engines – just clip on a new one and off you go. Swinging a massive diesel out of a yacht and replacing it with a new one is a heavy job that can often involve some major surgery to the cockpit sole, engine mountings and companionway.

Again, as an outboard can be detached and taken to a normal mechanic (at least four streets back from the marina), it is much cheaper to repair than calling a marine technician out to your boat at $80 an hour with no guarantee of success. The biggest bill Dan will ever receive is the $1200 it costs to replace the outboard entirely with a new unit that has a worldwide warranty. (He also gets to break down the old one and keep the good parts for spares). With repairs to a diesel, the sky is the limit.

It could be argued that a diesel is more economical over the long run, but if you are using it responsibly as we do, you would have to live for a very long time to feel the benefit. This statistic also assumes that a diesel will run until the end of its natural life, when in my experience, most die of some other cause well before they reach their four score and ten (usually from salt water ingress).

Space

As it lives on the transom, an outboard takes up no space inside the boat – an important consideration on a small vessel! The spare parts are also quite small.

Ken and Nancy and their 3 children on the 40ft Joe Adams designed *Magic*, sold their diesel engine and bought an outboard when they discovered their floating family was about to get larger. Rather than trade in their beloved boat (which the family built themselves) to accommodate the new addition to the crew, they simply turned the engine space into another cabin and rigged a bracket on the stern for an outboard.

Utility

Once safely anchored, the outboard can double up for use on the dinghy.

Simplicity

There is no need for holes in the boat for exhaust, cooling water or drive shaft. No engine alignment is necessary. No stuffing boxes or drip-less seals. No special laboratories are needed to calibrate injectors and fuel pumps.

Access

Engine access in small boats is notoriously awful and accounts for more foul language than all the celebrity chefs combined. Haul an outboard into the cockpit on a nice sunny day and you have great access to everything – you can invert it (drain the oil and petrol first!) turn it, lift it and ultimately carry it ashore if necessary and preserve your knuckles in the process.

Most of the objections I have heard to the outboard idea have come from people who use their diesels far too much. I entirely agree with them. If it is your intention to use your yacht as a motorboat with sails, then a big diesel is the only way to go. If however, it is your intention to sail everywhere and use your engine only when absolutely necessary, the outboard idea makes good sense – particularly for budget sailors.

One thing to consider is that petrol is a great deal more volatile than diesel. This is not an insurmountable problem, but you will have to make sure the storage is good. Many people who worry about having petrol aboard their boat wouldn't think twice about driving at 70mph with 200 litres of petrol nestled under the back seat in a thin, mild steel tank or having (the far more dangerous) propane tanks on board their boat for cooking, so I suspect much of the objection to be simple prejudice. If you intend to use your outboard sparingly, you will not need to store large amounts anyway. What trouble are you going to get into at 5mph with a 50 litre, 4mm thick stainless steel tank in a compartment that drains overboard?

It is also possible to disconnect completely your main fuel storage and just use a 'day tank', which you fill manually via a pump. This can reduce the danger should you have an engine fire. If the worst comes to the worst and there is an engine fire, at least it is not inside the bowels of the boat like the diesel – with a bit of clever thinking you may even be able to design a system that allows you to drop the whole thing in the water should the worst happen.

Storing petrol on board certainly needs some thinking about but much of the risk can be mitigated with good planning, practice and engineering.

3. Mike and Marie-France on *Dejala*

Mike and Marie-France have thrown the diesel overboard and replaced it with an electric motor. Where the fuel tank once lived, there is now a bank of nickel cadmium batteries that provide 20 hours of motoring before needing a recharge, which they achieve (of course) by solar panel and wind turbine. Naturally, having bought a good sailing boat and having the right attitude, they choose wind as their major form of propulsion – only switching on the electric motor for the last approach into a bay or harbour - and so never fully discharging their batteries, thus ensuring their longevity.

This is a fantastically low-tech green solution to the propulsion problem. Modern electric motors are light, reliable and much cheaper to replace than diesel engines. Mike and Marie-France even have a whole spare motor standing by which can be fitted in a matter of minutes. Electric motors are quieter, less smelly, require less cooling and never have starting problems. If you ever run out of fuel, just heave-to and wait for the sun to fill up your tank again. The batteries can double up as an amazing power source for your floating home when you are at anchor.

If you have the knowledge or have a friend who has, then this is an excellent way to go – but make sure you buy a boat that can actually sail and that you have a good commitment to travelling with the wind, or your motoring demands will be more than the system can provide which will result in a frustrating experience. This is why *getting real* is so important. With the wrong attitude, a wonderful, quiet, economical, green system like this can easily become a disappointment.

Generally then, a new sea gypsy really needs some kind of mechanical propulsion and you will probably inherit a diesel engine with the boat you buy. However, if you have got an amazing deal on your boat because the diesel engine is dead, then you have an opportunity to do something different. At the very least, you might consider replacing your diesel with a smaller, lighter one. It is the fashion these days to go for at least 3hp per metre as a rule of thumb, but this is far in excess of what a real sailboat needs as an auxiliary engine and is more a result of weekend yachtsmen getting richer and expecting to maintain 7 knots at all times in the right direction (time is money!) even in contrary winds.

The formula the marine industry uses to size a diesel engine (sometimes called the 'Kinney formula' after naval architect Francis S Kinney) starts with the assumption that you want to drive your boat for extended periods at full hull speed in all conditions. In other words, that you are a motor-sailor, not a sailor. This is quite an assumption!

Only 20 years ago, sailboats had nothing like this kind of engine power. Iconic budget sailors Annie and Pete Hill (after many years as engine-less sailors) decided to fit a diesel engine in their 34-foot junk rigged schooner *Badger*. Marine experts using the Kinney formula would recommend 35hp as the minimum requirement for that boat. The Hills fitted a 9hp, single cylinder Ducati engine and were very happy with it.

Our Norwegian friends Lisa and Shell on the 30ft Albin Ballard *Milla* are on their sixth year as ocean bashers with their trusty, 30 year old, Yanmar 8hp single cylinder diesel. This engine is so thrifty, they can actually motor for longer periods than boats with huge, thirsty engines despite storing significantly less fuel. It is also small enough to be started by hand cranking.

Unfortunately most experts today would consider both these boats to be seriously underpowered. As sailors get richer and manufacturers respond, the voices of moderation and good sense are increasingly overwhelmed by the juggernaut of marketing. What would have seemed excessive to everyone a few short years ago, now seems not just normal, but highly desirable - even essential - by 'experts' and dockside commentators alike. Fortunately for us, fashion and physics are not the same thing and there is no compulsion on your part to follow, simply because this is what everyone else does. Being different is really something one has to get used to in the sea gypsy life.

Whatever engine you end up with, make sure you know how to perform all the basic maintenance tasks. If you do not know how to bleed air out of your diesel, then simply running out of fuel or changing a filter will mean that you will be unable to re-start her. Marine diesels do not have much oil in the sump, so you can't afford to ignore the oil change schedule like you might in a car. The gates of nirvana will open to those who treat the manufacturer's maintenance schedule as the minimum requirement.

Another piece of advice that takes a bit of discipline to follow is this: If you buy a spare part, fit it immediately and keep the old one as a spare. Do not wait for the old part to break first. This has two major benefits. Firstly, you discover immediately whether you have been given the right part and that it is working correctly. This is particularly important for big ticket items as you can't take them back after they have been kicking around in the bilge for a year. If the part works fine, then great! It also means that you have a spare that you are 100% sure works and does not require any special tools you don't have on board to fit it.

Secondly, taking this pre-emptive approach reduces the risk that the part will fail at some less convenient moment (such as when you are about to pull off a truly impressive docking procedure with fake nonchalance while pretending not to have noticed the rather attractive spectators).

Each type of engine has its own service parts, but I always have aboard:

12 primary fuel filters

12 secondary fuel filters (diesels only)

12 tertiary fuel filters (diesels only)

12 oil filters (many outboards do not have oil filters)

8 oil changes

4 fan belts (not required on most outboards)

4 raw water impellers

2 spare injectors (spark plugs for outboards)

4 changes of gearbox oil

At least one spare hose of every size

At least four hose clips of every size

Emergency starting cord (outboards only)

Assorted nuts and bolts of the correct thread

Complete set of copper washers (diesel)

Gasket kits

I also have a few big ticket items like alternators and fuel pumps that I have picked up over the years, but the above list is a good place to start. I am amazed whenever I read of a boat whose engine has become 'disabled' due to a broken fan belt, impeller or any other 'problem' that would take all of 15 minutes to sort out given the right part. Even if you have no interest in mechanics, at least learn these simple tasks as the rest of us will feel pretty miffed if we have to put down our cold beer and come and do for you what any self-respecting seaman should be able to do for himself.

Chapter 13

The Curious Case of Self-Steering

Some form of self-steering is essential for all lightly crewed boats. Do not even consider voyaging as a single or a couple without it. Being chained to the helm is not only tedious, but prevents you from taking care of the boat's other myriad needs in a timely fashion. A boat that self-steers allows the crew to get good food and quality rest – not to mention all the other fun stuff a couple can get up to on their own yacht in the middle of the ocean. Furthermore, in my experience, even a really good helmsman can only concentrate fully for about forty-five minutes, less at night. Tired crew make bad decisions, are irritable at best and can easily turn mutinous.

So, for safety, efficiency, enjoyment and to reduce the risk of being set adrift in your own dinghy with only a nip of rum and a single bullet, put some form of self-steering on your 'must have' list.

In this era of Twitter, iPads and apps for everything, it seems almost inevitable that the solution to the steering problem should be technological - and indeed this is what you find on most production boats in the shape of an electronic autopilot.

Electronic autopilots are made up of five parts. A central computer receives information from an electronic compass and compares that information with the desired heading along with information from a sensor on the rudder. If they match, all well and good. If they don't match, the computer sends a signal to a powerful ram, which pushes the helm over until the course matches up again. This is all coordinated by a unit near the helm called the 'control head'.

As the sea is lumpy and non-uniform, the electric autopilot is constantly checking and correcting, working hard and pushing the rudder, this way and that. Seems like a good system eh?

Well no, not really. Apart from the power issue (power you probably don't have, particularly at night), electric autopilots have other disadvantages:

They don't like water.

This is all well and good when the sea is calm. For two years we happily used an electric autopilot on our boat *Calypso* in the relatively flat Sea of Cortez (where it rains about once per year). As soon as we left to cross the Pacific, the first wave in the cockpit drowned it for good.

Many manufacturers use terms like, 'splash proof' and 'water resistant', not in the hope of accurately describing their product's ability to withstand a good soaking, but to avoid using the term, 'waterproof' which has a whole different meaning in a legal sense and would make them liable for water damage.

They are not repairable by the average sea gypsy.

The fewer things that you have aboard that you are unable to repair, the happier you will be. Simple, but true.

They are expensive.

There are some cheap tiller pilots around, but to stand any

chance of steering your properly built cruising boat in rough seas, you will need something more powerful. (You can get away with using a cheap tiller pilot by hooking it up to a mechanical wind vane. We will discuss this later in Chapter 14).

They are very advanced in their marketing.

Manufacturers of electronic gear for boats are at the cutting edge of marketing. They both understand and employ modern marketing techniques such as fear, built in obsolescence, price differentiation, upgrade compulsion, consumer envy etc. For example, when our electric autopilot drowned itself at the first attempt, I called Simrad for a replacement control head and was told (perhaps predictably) that:

"This model is no longer made and the new control head is not compatible, so the whole system needs to be upgraded. The new model has so many more features and upgrading the system will give you many more benefits such as… blah, blah, blah…"

So a $500 dollar problem is now a $5000 problem and another term of private school fees for the director's kids. On top of that you have to listen to some salesman behaving as if he is improving your life while disembowelling your finances. Little wonder some people think sailing is so expensive! (Of course, being a sea gypsy, I did not upgrade the whole system, but managed to find a used part on ebay). I am not picking on Simrad particularly. I have had autopilots from other manufacturers and the story is always the same - barely able to resist the medium in which they work and calculatingly expensive to repair or replace.

They are noisy.

Nothing spoils the lovely sounds of the sea gurgling against your hull quite as well as the high pitched whine of an electric autopilot as it deviates, corrects, deviates, corrects...

They don't steer particularly well anyway.

Electric autopilots are all well and good on a calm sea, but I have yet to find one that steers reliably well in rougher conditions. Even if you do manage to hold a good course in lumpy conditions, the drain from the batteries is substantial. Furthermore, I find the way they steer rather frustrating. As a sailor, you can see a gust coming across the water from miles away and can take appropriate action to make the best of it. Even at night you can feel the wind increase on your face and react to it immediately. Using an electric autopilot is like watching your grandfather drive. You sit in the passenger seat with your foot pressed firmly on the imaginary controls because it is obvious he clearly hasn't seen the Volvo pulling out of the side street. Electric autopilots create the same feeling in the sailor because they are blind. Push them off course and they correct, but they cannot brace themselves or take pre-emptive action.

They steer a compass course.

Once you enter a course, your electric autopilot will try and hold that course whatever the wind does. This can often leave the boat improperly trimmed. A sudden wind change can cause a catastrophic gybe.

Some electronic autopilots have a wind setting, which allows you to set your course relative to the wind. For this (q'uelle surprise), you need more electronic gear – a wind sensor on the mast, a little box of electronics to display what it says, a 'NMEA sea talk' box (this is the protocol that most manufacturers use to get various electronic doo-dahs to talk to each other) and cables fitted all over the place (including one inside the mast itself) to relay the signal.

The mast sensor alone costs around $600 and lasts exactly as long as it takes for a pelican to land on it. When you try to replace it, you will probably be told that particular model is no longer made and you need to upgrade the whole system - and the happy caravan of cynical profiteering rolls on into another positive fiscal sunset on the wheels of your coin and the fuel of your frustration, while the innocent joy of sailing wilts in the desert heat of soul-less sales figures. (Sorry about that - don't know what came over me).

They can often lead to bad practice.

I can't remember how many times I have seen a helmsman hit the autopilot button because the boat is so badly balanced that his arms are falling off trying to keep her on course. With the other forms of self-steering we will discuss, a boat must be properly trimmed and balanced before they will work. Your boat should always be properly trimmed and balanced for reasons of safety and comfort. Pushing a button does seem awfully tempting though. Perhaps if you break your mast in the middle of the ocean, you can press 'control+alt+delete' and get a new one.

As you have probably guessed by now, I do not recommend electronic autopilots as a suitable way for a budget sailor (or any sailor for that matter) to go about getting her boat to self-steer on passage.

Yet getting your boat to self-steer is one of the most important aspects of seamanship for a lightly crewed boat. Fortunately it is possible to get your boat to self-steer without using complicated, power-hungry, accident-prone, electronic gadgets. The simplest and cheapest way of doing this is by using the forces in the sails and this is called, 'sheet to tiller'.

Sheet to Tiller

If you are smart enough to have bought a tiller-steered boat (a stick as opposed to a wheel), then firstly, well done! The tiller is a fabulously simple steering device, whereas a wheel is far more complicated, takes up space and needs maintaining. Don't even get me started on replacement costs. If the boat you want to buy has a wheel, it is not a deal-breaker, but a tiller is a much better option for the budget sailor.

Having a tiller also means that you can get your boat to steer herself in pretty much all conditions simply by attaching lines from the sails to the tiller and balancing those lines with bungee cord. I have made a short video about how this works on YouTube (the link is on our website).

Sheet to Tiller steering is such a rewarding and fascinating subject, that I have decided to devote a whole book to it. Email me if you would like to know when it becomes available.

Here, however are the basic bones of it.

The picture below shows how to get a boat to self-steer when close reaching (i.e., when you are heading into the wind, but not hard on it). The system changes with wind direction, so don't try this downwind!

First trim the sails of your boat until the helm is balanced (i.e., the boat is not trying to go upwind or downwind the moment you let the tiller go, but is easy to steer and if left unattended, turns slowly up to the wind). Set up your lines as per the diagram and loosen the main sheet so the tiller is being held in place by the balanced forces of the bungee and the control line. This takes a bit of fiddling about, but it is not so hard. Once you are steering a fairly straight course, watch the tiller and this is what you should see:

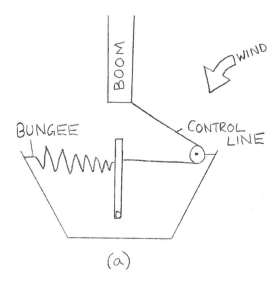

(a)

Fig a. Balanced boat, on course

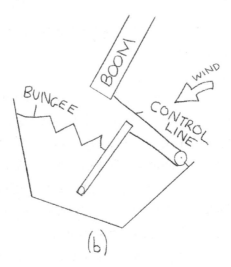

(b)

If the boat heads up to the wind, the pressure on the mainsail will increase as the apparent wind rises, overwhelming the force in the bungee cord, pulling the tiller to starboard and returning you to your course (fig b).

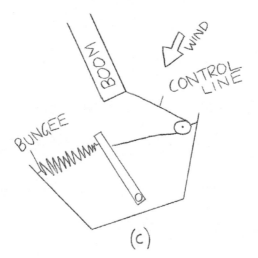

(c)

If your boat heads away from the wind, the pressure on the mainsail will decrease and the bungee cord will pull the tiller to port, sending you up to the wind again (fig c)

Once you have the knack, sheet to tiller has some great advantages over other systems:

It's cheap and fantastically simple!

You may need to buy the odd line and a couple of blocks or bungees, but most of what you need, you probably have on board right now.

It's repairable.

How hard is it to replace a worn bungee cord?

It's pre-emptive.

As discussed earlier, electronic steering systems only react to changes in direction – the boat is knocked off course by a wave or a gust, the computer compares the new course with the desired course and corrects. The result is that the boat describes a kind of S-shaped track across the water. With sheet to tiller, as soon as a gust hits your mainsail (or whatever sail you are attaching the control line to) the tiller reacts – turning the appropriate way before the boat has hardly had the time to round up.

Working to windward, sheet to tiller can be set up sensitively so that it will become extremely good at 'stealing a lift' (a technique used by sailors where they steer up closer to the wind during gusts when working to windward). This is just one of the many tricks you can do with sheet-to-tiller steering.

It is extremely rewarding.

Sheet to tiller is an exhaustive subject, but a fascinating one. There are a million ways of adjusting the forces in the control lines and the bungees on various points of sail. For me, nothing comes close to the pleasure of balancing all those forces successfully and watching my boat steer herself like she is on rails.

Unfortunately our current boat has a wheel (the next boat won't). However, I have had some promising results with a sheet to wheel converter (see picture below). This system uses removable pegs to independently adjust the radius described by the bungee and the control line. So far it is just a prototype but if I can get it to work well, I will update this chapter and post the results on the website. Drop me a line if you want to be kept posted. (I have no interest in patenting the design so if you want to have a stab at it, go ahead and let me know how it works out).

Wind Vane Self-Steering

There are several types of wind vane self-steering on the market. They all have their particular strengths and we will get to them in a moment.
For now, let us look at what they all have in common:

- They all use a vane (like a small sail) to detect changes in the angle of the wind relative to the boat and transfer that information to a blade in the water.

- They are mechanical (not electrical like autopilots).

- They can steer your boat 24 hours a day without using any fuel or electricity, just the wind and the action of the water.

- They are 100% green.

- They are totally silent.

- They are many times more reliable than an electronic autopilot.

- They are much easier to repair than an electronic autopilot and much less likely to need it.

- A cheap, low power, electronic tiller pilot can be used to operate the vane when you are motoring or when there is little wind. (see chapter 14 Electricity).

- You cannot drown them.

They are better than a third crew member because:

- They do not need to eat.

- They don't get tired.

- They do not use up fresh water.

- They do not talk back to the captain or make mutinous remarks.

- They do not flirt with the captain's main squeeze.

- They steer more reliably and never lose concentration.

- You cannot drown them.

If sheet to tiller is not right for you then you will need one of these when you are ready to head off voyaging. There are basically two types: the servo pendulum and the auxiliary rudder.

The auxiliary rudder system is the simplest, so we shall start there.

Basically, a wind vane picks up changes in the wind direction caused by your boat moving off course. That signal is transferred mechanically down to an independent rudder or a trim tab attached to the boat's usual rudder and this corrects the course.

The most popular vane of this type is the Hydrovane, built in the UK and Canada. The Hydrovane system is widely used and well proven, but quite expensive.

The servo pendulum is the most popular type of wind vane and develops the most steering power. Again, it works by using a vane to pick up changes in the wind direction relative to the boat. However, instead of transmitting that force straight to an independent rudder, it sends it to an oar that is in the water. This oar is turned and is now forced to one side or the other by the pressure of the sea moving over it. This motion is transferred by lines to the tiller or wheel and the course is thus corrected. Imagine putting your hand out of a car window with your palm horizontal so the wind is flowing equally over the back and palm of your hand. When you rotate your arm clockwise or anticlockwise, you can feel the force of the wind pushing your arm up or down. That is more or less how the servo-pendulum system works. (See picture below).

picture courtesy of Scanmar

The most popular servo pendulum systems are generally cheaper than the Hydrovane and develop a lot of steering power. In Europe, the Aries is a good choice and in the US, the Monitor is king.

We have a Cape Horn, which takes a little bit more fitting, but eliminates all lines in the cockpit and is extremely elegant, low maintenance and attractively priced. It is rare that I ever suggest spending money, so believe me when I say, don't even think about going voyaging without some form of mechanical self-steering.

The price tag can be a bit of a shock, but the good news is that you can often pick them up used. You will be amazed how many sailors of the iPhone generation remove them from their boats in favour of an electronic solution! You will have plenty of time to find and fit one because you will be somewhere beautiful, taking your time to learn about your boat and prepare her and yourselves for a time when you might want to go further afield. During this time, keep a weather eye out for a used one and then buy the service kit from the manufacturer.

IMPORTANT NOTE: The above advice is based on the idea that you eventually want to go voyaging. Only then do you really need mechanical self-steering. Remember though: There is no requirement for you to make long passages if you don't want to, just because other people (for some bizarre reason) expect it of you simply because you own a boat! There is little point in becoming a chilled out, uber-relaxed sea gypsy if you then feel pressurized to do something you are not ready for, or maybe don't want to do at all.

Plenty of watery wanderers cruise a small area where they are never more than a few hours from their next anchorage. If that is what works for you then go for it! Intimate knowledge of a smaller area brings a different, yet equally valid set of rewards. For many sailors, developing an in-depth understanding of a smaller geographical area, having local friends, getting to grips with the fish migrations and local culture is far more rewarding than marginal knowledge of a whole ocean. There is nothing particularly noble about struggle or distance. Don't let anybody's expectations set your agenda (or your limits) for you.

Remember our motto:

Smiles on deck, not miles under the keel.

Chapter 14

Staying Switched On – Electricity Aboard

Some purists say that there is no place for electricity on a boat and I admire them greatly and semi-agree with them. Salt water and electricity are a worse combination than rednecks and religion.

Having said that, there are certain things that I cannot live without, such as GPS (much more accurate and therefore safer than the old sextant), VHF radio, navigation lights and my beloved computer which Jasna and I both need to make a living as we voyage upon the big blue wobbly stuff. So, hats off and all due respect to the purists, but as in most things, a middle way is possible.

The problem that many sailors get into is one of importing habits learnt on land. When you live in a house and you need to buy another freezer, you get it home, stuff your husband's body in it, plug it in and voila! The new appliance simply draws more current from the grid and the only time you notice it is when the bill arrives and your angina kicks in.

On a boat, you must think of every amp and where it comes from. If you decide to add marine refrigeration, you cannot simply connect it to the batteries and call it a day. You will also have to find a way of putting that current into the batteries. This will mean more solar power, wind turbines, petrol generators or, god forbid, starting the diesel to charge the batteries.

There are few things quite as bad for your diesel engine as to be run without load just to charge the batteries. The picture below shows a piston from a marine diesel that had only been run for 500 hours. Next to it is a new one. All the pistons were virtually destroyed because the engine had been run primarily to charge the batteries. You will want to avoid this type of damage if you also want to avoid the substantial cost of replacing your engine.

So you must get your electrical power elsewhere, and the best source is the wind and the sun. Fortunately, this fits in nicely with the sea gypsy ethic as well as being extremely economical. Let's look at solar first.

Solar technology has leaped forward in recent years, particularly in the area of production, which has bought the price down considerably. They are silent, reliable and green as well – what is not to like? Some sailors claim that solar does not provide enough power for their needs, but this usually means their needs are too great or their panels are badly positioned.

It is not well known that for most solar panels, the slightest shadow can reduce performance by up to 90% - and all boats are full of shadows from rigging, mast, halyards etc. There are more expensive types of panel available where this problem has been somewhat mitigated, but even those will suffer to some extent from shadows and bad alignment to the sun. Generally then, to be effective, solar panels must be free from shadows and aligned with the sun.

When we first bought *Calypso* she had one 75Watt solar panel mounted on top of the radar arch (see picture). Apart from the shadow permanently cast by the backstay, the previous owner had then added a radar, a GPS antenna, a wind generator (not in shot) and a whip aerial. All of which cast shadows at some point during the day, reducing the efficiency of the panel to almost nothing. I can see where solar gets a bad rap from!

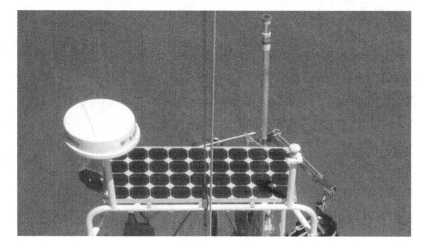

Now look at the next picture. Here you can see three 50W solar panels mounted on the rail and the bimini. They are mounted with brackets that open and can be tilted to face the sun and even swapped onto the other side of the boat to take full advantage of all those lovely solar amps free from space, whatever time of day it is.

With this method, we charge six batteries (one start battery and five deep-cycle), run all our computers and other luxuries (more on those later) without ever needing to start the engine. We achieve this with significantly less solar power than most would consider possible. The trick is not so much the total wattage, but to use what you have to its maximum advantage - and that means moving them to where they can suck up the most free energy for the longest possible time.

The brackets are readily available at most marine chandleries and I made the frames myself with $20 worth of flat aluminium bar stock from a double-glazing shop. For more tips on solar look in Nigel Calder's fantastic book (you are SO going to need a copy of this!) *The Boat Owner's Mechanical and Electrical Manual*. This is the sea gypsy's bible and one of the few things I won't sail without.

Wind Turbines

Wind turbines can also be useful, but with certain caveats. Firstly, they tend to be noisy and keep people awake. Secondly, many only start producing useful amounts of juice at around 15 knots. As most boats spend more than 80% of their time at anchor, then this can be a problem because most people choose their anchorages precisely because they don't have strong winds constantly howling through them.

However, when the sun is behind heavy clouds for a few days and the wind is blowing, a good wind generator will produce enough juice to satisfy the needs of hungrier boats than ours, so they can be a godsend.

If you decide to buy one, leave it until after you have done your solar installation. Also, buy one that produces current at low wind speeds. Take advice from other sailors because the performance figures from the manufacturers are misleading to the point of farcical.

For example, the company Airex who make one of the more popular wind generators, give their output figures in amps without specifying what the voltage is at the time. Not to get too technical here, but a generator can produce a gazillion amps but not a single one of them will pass into your batteries unless the voltage it also produces is greater than the voltage of the batteries (which for a 12v battery is usually a shade under 13v).

As there is no industry standard for describing wind turbines, the manufacturers are practically free to imply anything they want. I hated my Airex and found it produced very little aside from noise and nerves (it screamed like a demented witch when the wind piped up to the point where it might actually be of any use). We now have a Ferris 200 which (by dint of its large blade size) starts producing current at much lower wind speeds and is relatively quiet too (although some snobby yachtsmen have commented that it looks like it belongs on a barn). I have also heard good things about the KISS wind generator as well, but have no direct experience of it.

Of course, being designed for the marine environment means that they are expensive. I have met a few sailors who use various non-marine wind generators (designed for 'coastal installations') with great success. As these generators are not being targeted specifically towards the (supposedly) wealthy marine environment they are of course, less than half the price.

Cutting Requirement

Many boats you will see for sale often seem to have enough power for the things on board, but it is a mistake to accept that this is the case, particularly a boat that lives in a marina where batteries can be charged each night from the mains supply. Even those boats with solar panels may not have enough power (or power storage) to supply their needs without starting their engines for a couple of hours every evening and morning. This is particularly true if they are running marine refrigeration and freezers.

The less electricity you need, the easier it is to harvest it from the sun and wind. If you can keep the electrical demands of your floating home to a reasonable level, then you will not need to run your engine, buy a generator, or go to a marina simply to charge your batteries. The easiest way to do this of course is to take a good look at what you don't need and get rid of it. A good place to start is with the expensive, unreliable stuff.

You only need to spend ten minutes in the company of sailors who have just crossed an ocean to know that the same three items cause the majority of electrical problems on cruising boats. Rather than chuck these things overboard, their owners (having now become dependent upon them) spend all their time in paradise trying to repair them, ordering parts for them from abroad and negotiating the often torturous labyrinths of customs and excise in a largely unknown language. We know this because we watch them pulling their hair out from aboard our uncomplicated little cutter *Calypso,* but many formal studies confirm it. These three items (in order of most annoying) are water makers, electronic autopilots and fridges.

Water makers

The water maker is the number one pain in the arse piece of electrical equipment on a boat (with the electric autopilot coming a very close second). They are temperamental, difficult to repair, have high power demands and are only really necessary for passenger vessels or for those who intend to continue consuming fresh water at the same catastrophic rate they did on land. Why not learn to conserve? Why not shower in salt water and keep your precious fresh water for the rinse? How about catching some rain or jumping overboard? Heaven forbid you would take your plastic jerry cans into a village and actually talk to some local people! Furthermore, few boats have the solar capacity to run water makers without then starting the engine or the generator to top up the batteries, so they are not particularly green either. (I have heard several sailors claim that they run their water maker purely on solar, only to hear them start the generator later in the evening. They don't seem to make the connection between the two actions because they happen at different times).

In short then, water makers are expensive to buy, expensive to maintain (impossible in remote areas), isolate you from local communities, consume huge amounts of power and require specialized parts that are difficult, often impossible, to get hold of.

Electric Autopilot

Not surprisingly, electric autopilots cause nearly as many headaches as water makers. They are complicated, expensive to buy and expensive to replace. Built-in obsolescence often means that if one part breaks, you will have to replace the whole system. (This can be a disaster if this is the primary method you have for steering your boat. However, this is not the disaster for us sea gypsies as it is for other sailors because for us, an electric autopilot is just a luxury occasionally used while motoring. As sea gypsies of course, we have some form of mechanical self-steering, so we carry on as though nothing has happened).

Apart form being vulnerable, fragile, unreliable and expensive, electric autopilots draw a fair amount of power – particularly steering in difficult conditions, where they are often fighting large forces. If you have followed the advice in chapter 13 and the wind is controlling your direction via a mechanical self-steering system, then none of this is a problem. However, what do you do if the wind is too light to steer the boat or you need to motor a long distance in a flat calm?

Here is where wind vane self-steering can help again. Instead of buying a $5000 autopilot strong enough to steer the boat directly, buy a cheap $400 self-contained tiller pilot (see our website) and connect it to the vane of the wind vane self-steering. When there is no wind, you can flip it on and it will steer your boat. The wind vane steering gear is still providing the power to steer (which is why you can use the smallest, cheapest tiller pilot you can find) while the tiller pilot is simply providing the signal formerly provided by the wind. Now you can happily motor on autopilot or sail in very light airs that are not strong enough to activate the wind vane - for a fraction of the cost, liability and power drain of the dedicated electric autopilot.

Furthermore these little units are self-contained, so you are not tied to any particular manufacturer. Should you need to replace it, the manufacturer cannot manipulate you with built-in obsolescence to buy a load of expensive stuff you don't want. You simply tell them to shove it, and buy a different model from another manufacturer.

Fridges and Freezers

We have lived much of our on board life without marine refrigeration with no problem. If you don't have the solar capacity, so will you. The fridge is normally the biggest drain on electrical power on a boat and living without one will pretty much solve most power issues. This is not the problem it might at first seem as there are plenty of ways to preserve food that do not involve cooling it (see chapter 18). However, nothing beats a cold beer or an icy cocktail in the tropics and buying ice every few days gets expensive and is often unavailable, so let's have a look at ways to cut the power drainage and the expense of marine refrigeration.

The marine fridge technician in La Paz charges $100 an hour (whether he fixes it or not) and that is in the relatively cheap environment of Mexico. My doctor in Mexico charges me $4 for a half-hour consultation, so you can see what an easy life many marine professionals are making for themselves at our expense. God knows what his counterpart in Monaco hopes to receive for similar services. Either way, the marine refrigeration technician is a guy you hope to never need. The simplest and cheapest solution we found on our first boat *Marutji* was to buy one of the portable 12v fridges built for the RV industry and some bottles of water.

For $250 we bought a decent size fridge and built a wooden

harness for it inside *Marutji*. For good measure, we chucked some extra insulation around it as well. During the day, when there is normally an excess of power from the solar panels, we ran it flat out to cool the food and the bottles of water (you can also use those blue blocks which are even more efficient). At night, we would switch it off to spare the batteries and the cold or frozen water bottles would stop the temp from rising too much until the sun came out the following day and power was restored. Because we have a good wind turbine, we would leave the fridge on overnight if there was any kind of breeze blowing. We always switched the fridge on when the engine was running anyway (i.e., when we were using the engine to drive the boat).

This technique can allow you to run a fridge without too much strain on your electrical system. Two further advantages to this system are that;

- **You never need to meet the marine refrigeration technician**. Because your fridge is not permanently plumbed into your boat, you can simply lift it out and take it to a domestic repair shop (at least four streets back from the marina) and get it fixed for a fraction of the price.

- **Your fridge cannot bankrupt you**. At $100 an hour, your marine fridge can repeatedly cost you a fortune.

Imagine the tech has just spent 5 hours fixing your problem and you have handed over $500 (plus parts and tax) and sailed off into the sunset. You are now a thousand miles downwind and the fridge craps out again and seems as likely to work as a teenager contemplating exam revision. Are you going to beat back a thousand miles just to make a probably futile attempt at reimbursement?

Of course not.

You will have to suck it up and bend over for the next marine professional (who will no doubt blame the last one) and fork over more cash for similarly unguaranteed services. Repeat ad nauseum, until broke or thoroughly disillusioned.

If you have a little $250 RV fridge (of the type made by Waeco) then the worst bill you can ever get is $250 - and for this you get a new unit with a worldwide guarantee – not some antique unit patched up by largely unqualified 'professionals'.

Calypso had a relatively reliable fridge when we bought her and this might be the case for you too. In this case, like us, you may decide to use it until it breaks down. We currently run our fridge (still using water bottles to keep it cool at night so as not to strain the batteries) without too much trouble. The fridge is getting old now and starting to misbehave and we will be replacing her with an RV model as soon as it becomes problematic.

Don't even think about freezers[14].

---

[14] Since writing this, the fridge has finally packed up and we simply learnt to live without it. Within 2 weeks we had forgotten we ever had one. We are enjoying having more spare power than we know what to do with. So pop on over if you see us and charge up your smart phone. Just don't expect a cold beer.

Further tips on reducing power consumption

The three examples above are the main culprits and most boats can resolve their power issues by addressing them. However, there are many other things you can do to further reduce your power needs.

LEDs (Light Emitting Diodes).

LEDs have come a long way in recent years and no longer have to produce the stark light of a mortuary if you choose 'warm white' over 'hard white'. They are now even powerful enough to use as anchor and navigation lights (which must be visible for two miles). They are relatively cheap, last for ages and consume very little power.

Avoid inverters.

Inverters take the 12volt supply from your battery and convert it to normal domestic 240v mains supply (110v in the US). It is useful to have an inverter should you need to use your power tools on board, but do not rely on them for the gadgets you use every day as they put strain on the batteries and waste energy. Furthermore, in the majority of cases, this wastage is completely unnecessary. Your phone charger, for example, probably needs less than 5 volts. When you plug it into a 240v supply at home, that little box on the cable converts the 240v down to 5v and gets hot in the process. All that heat is wasted energy. What is the point in asking your boat's battery to step up to 240v and then asking your phone charger to step it back down to 5v again? Both conversions will cost energy and create heat. Maybe it is not hot enough in your boat already? Instead, install 12v 'cigarette lighter' sockets all over your boat, buy the car charger for your phone and cut out the waste. The same goes for virtually every electronic device you can think of – laptops, tablets, stereos, iPods, cameras, kindles – all of them need less than 12 volts (some laptops need a little more, so bear that in mind when buying one. Don't despair if you already have an 18v laptop as there are 12v chargers for those too which, while a little more hungry, are still much thriftier than inverting all the way up to 240v and then back down to 18v). It almost goes without saying that for music, a car stereo is best as it is already designed to run on 12volts.

Generally then, buy the 12 volt car charger rather than use the inverter and your batteries will love you.

NOTE: I am aware that it is possible to buy little inverters that fit in cigarette lighter sockets, which you then plug your normal AC power supply into. However, we have had two of these and they have been responsible for the only two fires we have had on board (as they try and suck way too much power through the thin wires that 12v sockets are usually connected with) *and* they still suck up more power than the 12v option. From now on, don't buy anything electronic that does not have the facility to be powered or charged from a 12volt supply!

When it is raining outside, we love to curl up with a glass of wine and a movie. We even have a flat screen TV! (I bet that surprised you). What you may not know is that most flat screen TVs are very energy efficient. Most of them run on 12v or 19v and need a little box (just like the one on your phone charger) to drop the domestic voltage from 240v to 12v or 19v.

Buy a normal 240v (or 110v in the US) TV that really only needs 12v (the specs are written on the unit), take the little box out and you have a marine TV! Ours cost $100, 3 years ago, uses little energy and is still going strong. We did have a little problem with it when we first bought it caused by some idiot (ahem!) connecting it up the wrong way after removing the little box. But because we were able to take it a couple of streets back from the marina to a normal television repair shop (as opposed to having a 'marine electronics expert' – or 'licensed bandit with a voltmeter' as they are often called - come to the boat) the repair cost only $20 and I was able to hide my stupidity from Jasna for yet another week.

As I said at the beginning of this chapter, I admire very much people like the Pardeys who have no electrical stuff on board at all – they use oil lamps for lighting and navigation and do not have a transmitting radio. I also admire Hussein Bolt, but that does not mean I can run the 100m in under 10 seconds. I am, like most sailors, not nearly as dedicated to purist sailing as I could be. I love my little luxuries - a nice sounding stereo, a movie and a glass of wine curled up with my lovely wife in a snug anchorage on a rainy Sunday afternoon and a decent laptop and camera to earn my living on.

Does this mean that we have to sign up for the great consumer-binge that is yacht marketing today? Not at all. With the right attitude and a little organisation, you can most definitely find a workable balance. There is at least a little wheat in all that chaff and the trick is to find it. There is an enormous amount of difference between a 12v laptop that draws little current directly from a 12 volt supply, and a washing machine that needs massive amounts of power from a generator, engine or a rack of electrically inverted batteries and tens of gallons of water from a generator-powered water maker to perform a function that we could easily perform for ourselves. In fact, washing machines deserve a special mention because their existence on boats brings into embossed relief the wrong attitude to bring to electricity in your new sea gypsy life.

Washing Machines

A washing machine works on electricity, which must be produced by a generator or by running your main engine (solar rarely produces enough power, even if you could find a washing machine that functioned directly from a 12volt supply). Whatever generation system you use will need fuel, spares, servicing, repairs and eventual replacement at intervals many times shorter than their land-based counterparts. The same goes for the washing machine itself. Furthermore, washing machines consume huge amounts of precious fresh water which means either, you need massive water tanks or, (cross yourself when you say it), a water maker and all the power requirements, spares and repairs for that expensive little toy as well as its ultimate replacement.

The above is enough justification for throwing it over the side – particularly as you will have a lot less laundry than you did on land (unless of course you are not sailing at all, but living in the marina and dressing for dinner every night in the restaurant - in which case you are most definitely holding the wrong book). But perhaps, the real madness of having a washing machine on board only becomes obvious when you stop and think what a washing machine actually does.

A washing machine is a device for agitating water.

You are living on the rolling ocean and the only way you can think to agitate water is to spend thousands and thousands of dollars on complex, unreliable machinery (and all the generators, water makers, marine professionals and spares to run it)? Really? The ridiculousness of this demonstrates most clearly how marketing has taken control of our brains. It might surprise you to learn then, that we have a washing machine onboard *Calypso*. Here is a picture of it.

This 60 litre tub once contained chemical fertilizer and is very tough. You can also use beer-brewing barrels – anything tough that has a screw down or clip-on lid. Simply pop your wash into the barrel with some water you have caught from a recent downpour, drop in a couple of round rocks (we use wooden balls with stainless steel inserts to make them neutrally buoyant). Add some washing powder, screw on the lid and go sailing. The motion of the boat will produce exactly the same effect as an electric washing machine.

After a couple of hours drain the water (we have a tap in the base of ours which cost $3) and add some more for the rinse. Voila. Every bit as good as a complicated washing machine, but it cost $23, is 100% reliable, requires no spares, no 'marine professionals', no electricity, no generators and can be replaced in an afternoon for the cost of a round of beers. It is also smaller and lighter than its electric counterpart for the same size washing load and uses much, much less water, so no water maker is required either.

Sure, it can't spin dry, but you live on a boat in an anchorage. There is wind to dry your clothes and plenty of lines to hang them from. Furthermore, if you hang your clothes out wet rather than spin drying them, they don't need ironing. So you can throw the iron over the side as well.

When not in use as a washing machine, we use it to store our 'grab bag' because it is buoyant, waterproof, easily spotted and can be ditched over the side and into the life raft in an instant. Try doing that with a Sudz-o-Matic 600.

You see how washing machines are the epitome of madness? With wave energy free, simple, green and on our doorstep, the only benefit offered by the fantastically hi-tech, expensive, annoyingly unreliable system of watermaker/generator/ washing machine, is the illusion that you are still at home in your apartment and connected to all the services.

The washing machine is 100% illusion, yet all unnecessary marine products are at least partly illusion, the trick is to spot them before they suck you in. So set your bullshit detector to 'kill' when you go shopping for electrical stuff.

It is much easier, cheaper and ultimately more rewarding to adapt to your new life than to try and create a floating version of your old one.

Chapter 15

Staying on Course – Budget Navigation

(The consumer juggernaut rolls on)

As we have hopefully established by now, yachting is big business. We all know the popular image of the private surgeon who has a picture of his 72ft racing yacht *Flash Bastard* on the wall of his consulting rooms, which he steals dreamy glances at whilst nonchalantly presenting you with your massive bill for a routine tonsillectomy that took all of twenty minutes. I am pleased to say that most sailors do not fit this stereotype, but there is no smoke without fire.

There is a huge market of over-moneyed yacht owners out there - and where there is money, there is marketing. Nowhere is this more readily apparent than in the field of electronic navigation gizmos, which get flashier every year and are yet another example of the triumph of money over sense. The same type of person who ashore must have the latest telephone is often the nautical fool who must constantly replace all his electronics. This profligate and environmentally irresponsible attitude sometimes wears a false mask of respectability by referring to itself as 'upgrading'. I suppose upgrading sounds better that 'wasting'.

There are only two ways to sell something: fill a need or create a need and then fill it. How do you create a need? Fear, desire, avarice. Tell someone that they are in danger or they are not proper sailors without the latest gizmo and they will start looking for their credit card.

Many electronic companies are huge and employ professional marketers who have no idea of what the sea is like, but are great salesmen.

"Don't leave harbour without it" is generally the attitude they take.

This type of fear generation is becoming so universal that I recently heard somebody say that, "anyone who goes to sea in a boat of less than 50 feet is asking to die".

Ignoring for a moment that many of the legendary sailors like Joshua Slocum, Bernard Moitessier, Robin Knox Johnson, The Pardeys, the Hiscocks and numerous others all circled the globe for decades in boats well under 50 feet (the Pardeys' boat was under half of that!), this sailor had clearly allowed snobbery and fear-based marketing to define his judgement. Why let the facts get in the way of a great marketing campaign and corporate profits?

There is however, a silver lining in this cloud. The orgy of flashing gizmos on the market and over-moneyed sailors daft enough to constantly upgrade them, means that the few things that you actually need can be bought used, or at least more cheaply if you stay away from the 'latest' models.

So here it is, the sea gypsy's guide to essential navigation stuff:

Compass

Preferably gimbaled, lit and mounted where it can be seen from the helm. Having said that, I know of at least one circumnavigator who uses a cheap car compass that he picked up in a service station for a few dollars. However, in our opinion, a good compass is worth the money.

GPS

A sextant is a wonderful thing, but prone to user error, easily damaged, inaccurate on a pitching, rolling deck and impossible on cloudy days. Many traditional sailors still use a sextant exclusively, but there is no case for it unless, like us, you actually enjoy being a bit of a luddite beardy-weirdy. If you are (quite rightly) concerned about losing electrical power, then buy a few spare handheld GPS units and a heap of batteries (they are only $50 each now. Soon they will be giving them away with Coco Pops). Put at least one inside a steel box in case of lightning strike.

On *Calypso* we have seven independent GPS systems including one that is inside two steel boxes, which we then chuck in the oven (another steel box) when we see lightning on the horizon. If you still feel a little vulnerable, then you can pick up a cheap sextant on ebay as a back-up for a couple of hundred dollars and learn how to use it whilst growing a big bushy beard. We like sextants, but neither of us can grow a decent beard, so we will never be truly expert with them.

Paper Charts

So, you have been hit by lightning and all you have left is your hand-held GPS (which you were smart enough to wrap in foil and store in a metal container) or your sextant, which you have prudently learnt to use. Bravo! Take a moment to pat yourself on the back for being better prepared than most boats. However none of this preparation will do you a scrap of good if you don't have a paper chart to plot your position on.

Without paper charts, GPS coordinates might as well be your lottery numbers. The law no longer requires large commercial vessels to carry paper charts and this has led some sailors to claim (and even publish, I am ashamed to say) that small boat sailors do not need to carry them either. This is nonsense for two reasons.

Firstly, sailing boats are comparatively vulnerable to relatively small waves finding their way aboard and knocking out their electronics. If the sea is ever bad enough to swamp the bridge of a super-tanker, then her position is probably the least of her worries.

Secondly (and most importantly) all commercial vessels follow established shipping routes, which are programmed into their computers. They rarely have to deviate due to unfavourable winds (because they are all diesel powered) and generally don't go off exploring backwaters or picnicking up rivers. On the rare occasions that they are forced to deviate from the shipping lane routes, they use their iridium telephone to advise their employers who can check the new route against the latest paper charts.

Us sailors can never predict the actual course we will take because we cannot predict the wind or sea conditions accurately for more than a few days ahead. Furthermore, our routes are infinitely more varied than the average commercial vessel and we do not have a team of marine professionals an iridium phone call away who are keen to protect their multi-million dollar investment.

Therefore, don't let the exception the commercial vessels have managed to lobby for themselves lull you into a false sense of security.

Every few months there seems to be a new report of a yacht hitting reefs or rocks that were not visible on the electronic chart, but quite clearly marked on the paper one. The photograph below shows the opposite situation – the electronic chart indicates that *Calypso* is sailing over land. She is a great boat admittedly, but not so great that she can nip ashore and pick me up a latte.

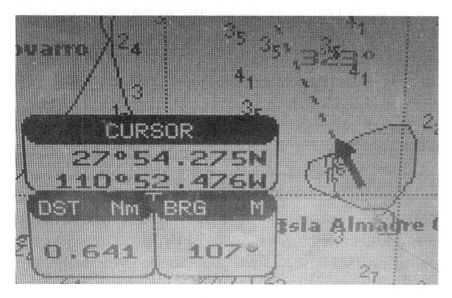

Being able to plot your position on a paper chart at any time is a matter of safety. We know of too many boats that were hit by lightning and lost all of their electronics to think that it could never happen to us. Those 56 charts in our chart table, emergency GPS, back up sextant and our trusty compass (and spare!) make us feel a whole lot better when we hear the rumble of thunder in the distance.

However, a heap of paper charts can be fantastically expensive and a little outsized for the pockets of many budget-minded sailors. Fortunately, many can be bought second hand, swapped with fellow sailors or copied (some are copyright protected and some are not, so if this type of thing concerns you, you had better check first).

I will never forget the day when I (Jasna) went to do the massive job of copying the paper charts for the whole Pacific Ocean. We were in Puerto Vallarta in Mexico, where an ex-sea gypsy had set up a free chart library (may Neptune bless him!). First I had to examine hundreds of charts to find those that we needed. Then I had to jump on a hot, crowded bus carrying those 40 huge sheets of paper and find a copy shop that had huge machines. Then back on the bus, to the library to return the originals, then another bus to the bus station – you get the idea.

At the end of the day I was totally exhausted and partially cooked, but it was worth it. Now we relax in the knowledge that wherever we go in the South Pacific, we always have the right chart. (NOTE: Be careful about copying from copies as you start introducing cumulative errors in much the same way as in-breeding does).

An Extreme Case

Kayaking back to *Calypso* that evening, I met a young couple on a tiny boat. They were getting ready to sail to Hawaii. I asked them if they wanted to copy any of our charts and their answer was:

"No, we don't bother with paper or electronic charts. We don't need them because we have the Google Earth app on our iPad".

This is not being a budget sailor, this is just plain stupidity and it is only by the grace of Poseidon that they made it to Hawaii.

You should never go to sea without some kind of chart. Neither your eyes nor Google Earth will be able to spot an underwater rock or reef at night and someone else will have to put themselves in danger to rescue you when you hit it.

Many sailors will claim that it is irresponsible to use old charts, but that is pure phooey. The real danger lies in trusting your chart to be perfect because it is new. All charts are out of date by the time they hit the shops and should be treated as such. All the important bits haven't moved since Captain Cook surveyed them and the rest of the changes are available free on the internet, so buy yourself a fine-nibbed pen and make the alterations yourself.

So now you have your copied, altered charts, don't forget to plot your position on them every hour or they might as well be Greek Government Bonds.

Electronic Charts

I bet that surprised you! We are not total luddites and electronic charts are a great source of information. You can buy a cheap chart plotter (ours was $100 on ebay and is still going strong after 5 years) or you can easily turn your laptop into a chart plotter with the addition of a $15 dollar GPS (some laptops like the Sony Vaio have a GPS built in to them) and some free software from the wonderful people at Open CPN (http://opencpn.org/ocpn/). If you have a tablet with GPS, then the Navionic charts are good value and usually quite accurate.

The trick to using electronic charts is to always doubt them. Plotting your position on the paper chart (if you haven't guessed by now) is essential and failure to do it is just plain slack seamanship.

Electronic chart plotters are quite useful for gauging leeway and drift. For example, if you set your estimated course by compass and plot your position on the paper chart, it might be several hours until your next plot shows that leeway and current have actually set you on a much different course than your estimate, and all that ground will have to be made up. An electronic chart plotter shows you immediately where you are heading and you can correct immediately. Chart plotters can also provide useful information on tides, currents, moon cycles and close-up diagrams of ports and harbours. Just always remember – never completely trust electronic charts. Forget this and you may end up like this hapless French sailor:

Patrice

It was a beautiful sunny afternoon in the bay of La Paz, Baja California. A stiff breeze was taking the sting out of the Mexican summer and I was relaxing in our shady cockpit, watching a sailboat with a big headsail full of wind barrelling into the anchorage. After a few moments, I realized that the boat had stopped moving.

"Hey, sweetie" I called to Rick through the companionway, "we have another boat on the sandbar."

There is a big spit of sand that separates the lively town of La Paz from the anchorage. This obstruction lies just under the water and is not visible to the naked eye. It is, however, clearly shown on all the paper charts and in every nautical guide. Yet, each week another boat needs to be pulled of it.

So, we hopped in the dinghy and spent the next hour getting the French single-hander back into deeper water. It was quite a scene, with Rick leaping on the boat to raise the mainsail (in order to make the boat heel over and therefore lift the keel a little higher in the water) and me in the dinghy pulling a halyard (from the top of the boat's mast) to tilt the stricken vessel even more. When the boat finally got off the sand, she flew away at 8 knots with me still holding the halyard and zipping along in our tiny dinghy. The last time our little dinghy had gone that fast, it was being delivered in a truck.

After helping the shell-shocked, ashen-faced Patrice drop his sails and anchor his boat in deeper water, we explained how to avoid the sand spit in future. He looked almost indignant.

"There is no sandbar there. Look!" he said, producing his iPad to prove it.

Rick refused to even look at the screen. Instead, he looked Patrice in the eye and said:

"How can you say there is no sandbar there? You just hit the bloody thing!" (By the way Patrice, if you are reading this we are still waiting for the bottle of rum you promised us).

Sadly, Patrice is not the only one. There are plenty of boats that end their dreams on a reef, which is not visible at certain magnifications on the electronic charts. Electronic chart companies realize this and get away with it by writing 'not intended for navigation' on their charts. So, if you haven't got the message yet, paper is king. If you learn only this, then this book has been worth the money.

Cruising Guides

As we have stressed in previous chapters, when you first embark on your new life as a watery wanderer, it makes more sense to pick an area you like and learn your seamanship and how your boat handles in local waters, rather than buy a boat at the boat show and push off around the world, fixing all the nasty surprises on the way. This approach has the added advantage of allowing you to buy the things you need over a longer time period. If you have (quite sensibly!) chosen the path advocated by this book, you will have all the time in the world to pick up things at boat jumbles, other sailors, sales, etc. Ain't life sweet?

One of the costs you can kick down the road is the kings's ransom you need for a big heap of new paper charts.

Say you have decided to buy a boat in the Virgin Islands (thumpingly good idea by the way). You can get away with a broad paper chart of your immediate area and a good cruising guide that shows all the anchorages in detail. Again, these are rarely cheap but always worth the investment as they give great detail about the local anchorages from a sailor's point of view. Just about every area has a cruising guide: *Charlie's Charts* for Polynesia, *Alan Lucas* for Australia, *Nancy Scott* for the Virgin Islands and so on. There are also plenty of electronic books, which have the advantage of being constantly updated. Our friends Eric and Sherrell on s/v *Sarana* for example have produced two fabulous guides for Central America. Once you pay your $13, you can download future updates free of charge, so they are always fairly current (see www.svsarana.com),

A couple of paper charts of your local area and the cruising guide is all you really need to get started. You can start amassing more charts if and when you decide to travel further afield.

Depth Sounder

If you only buy one electronic gizmo, make sure it is a depth sounder. It might sound romantic having someone on the bow checking the depth with a lead weight on a piece of string shouting, "17 feet sand and broken shell sir!", but it may not be practical - particularly for short handed (singles or couples) crews who will have other things to do at anchoring time. Depth sounders are fairly reliable, not too expensive and the only truly indispensable electronic navigation instrument. Most depth sounders give you the depth below your boat, which is fine. However, forward-looking depth sounders are becoming increasingly affordable and will give you the depth several meters in front of the boat, which, obviously, might be useful for avoiding sudden changes in depth, reefs or sleeping krakens. If you have inherited the normal 'straight down' depth sounder with your boat and it appears reliable, that is fine. Millions of boats worldwide use them and you do not need to add to the ever increasing amount of plastic in the ocean by 'upgrading'. (See chapter 11 for more on depth sounders).

VHF Radio

Most boats use VHF radio to communicate short distances (the best we have managed is 27 miles at sea, but don't expect that performance closer to land). Most boats (including the coastguard) monitor channel 16 and being able to contact them in an emergency might save your bacon. Furthermore, wherever there is a community of sailors (or more than three Americans, who always seem to be fabulously well organised) there is usually a sailors' 'net'.

A net is simply a time and place on the radio where local sailors can meet and share advice. This helps foster a sense of community amongst wildly different people and can be a hive of information for the sailor just arrived from elsewhere. Weather, local services, boat jumbles and other social events are often broadcast on the local net.

If your boat does not already have a VHF radio and you don't want to spring for one or fit the cable inside the mast, then for less than $200 you can buy a pretty good, 12v rechargeable, hand-held VHF. They do not have quite the range of a fixed VHF, but do offer the advantage of portability.

In his riveting book *Adrift,* Steve Callahan details the time he spent alone in a life raft before making landfall on Guadeloupe. He claims that he would have been rescued within days if he could have swapped his flares for a hand-held VHF to contact the many boats that sailed past him. That is certainly worth remembering and we have a hand-held VHF and a gazillion batteries in our grab bag. I would much prefer to spend just a few days of my life in a raft - rather than the 76 days that Mr Callahan endured. It would make a rubbish book though.

That's it! That is all you really need to get started (along with the lights and noise makers required by the law in your area which will probably already be on the boat when you buy it).

There is a whole lot more on the market and I have detailed below some of the other things you may be offered or might already be on the boat you buy. But make no mistake, the above is all you really need and some purists would say that even that small selection is excessive. Famous cruising couple and authors Lin and Larry Pardey do not have a chart plotter, a GPS or a transmitting radio. Neither Bernard Moitessier, the Hills nor the Hiscocks had anything like the amount of electronics on board I am recommending here, so the above list is long way from being an extreme view. My list includes a few more items than these admirably purist sailors because I am assuming that you are not an experienced mariner (or married to one) and you will have enough to learn in your new life without making things more difficult by having to master celestial navigation before you get started. These electronic devices are quite reliable, simple to use and represent solid value for money in a cost/benefit sense – particularly if you buy a model that has just been made obsolete by flash gizmo 2.0.

Finally, to reap the benefits on offer to today's sailor, it is important not to become polarised by opinion. We do not need to come down on any particular side in the continuing debate of traditional seamanship v modern technology. By taking the best of traditional seamanship (paper charts, emergency sextant and physical watch-keeping) and combining it with the best of modern technology (several independent GPS systems including one protected from lightning and an electronic chart plotter), you will have the safest system that has ever been available to navigators – and who could be unhappy about that?

Other Quite Good Navigation Stuff That You Can Live Without.

As long as you have got the stuff above, you can go virtually anywhere in the world. There are plenty of other things to spend your money on, but the items listed above are all you really need. If you find yourself flush with cash and want to add to your toys, first read chapter 10, *Sustainability*. If you are still determined to add some more nav stuff, here are some suggestions.

Radar

There is no doubt that radar can be useful, particularly in poor visibility. But most things that radar can do, you can do yourself by heaving-to, double checking your position and using your eyes. Radar can be useful for spotting squalls at night, but if you have reefed down as you should at night, then you only need to roll up the headsail when you feel the wind picking up and heave-to anyway.

I have also noticed that the addition of radar is encouraging bad practice amongst some sailors. Skippers that would have normally employed the solid seamanship of waiting for dawn before entering a harbour, are now feeling emboldened by the radar image to give it a go at night and often coming a cropper.

Furthermore, the alarm function on radar (it beeps when something comes into range) can encourage a bit of dozing on watch, which is fine while it works, but radar cannot see whales, reefs, rocks or small boats.

I am not saying that radar does not provide some useful information, but it is not a substitute for good seamanship. Furthermore, it is expensive and drinks a lot of power at exactly the time you have to conserve it (night). We inherited a radar with *Calypso*. At night the radar is often left in standby mode and only switched on to confirm the existence of something that has already aroused the suspicions of the watch through the good seamanship of physical watch-keeping. It is nice to have that extra confirmation, but remember:

All the great circumnavigators did it without radar and so can you.

AIS

A good alternative to radar for the budget sailor is the AIS system. All large commercial vessels are required to broadcast their name, position and heading via the AIS system. Just a few years ago the gear needed to receive those signals was prohibitively expensive. Today, companies like Standard Horizon provide AIS information with their VHF radios (see our website). So if you don't have a VHF radio yet, this is a good way of killing three birds with one stone.

AIS has some advantages over radar. Firstly, it is much cheaper to buy and maintain. Secondly, AIS uses a fraction of the power of radar, and thirdly, AIS provides you with the name of the vessel heading your way. It is my experience and that of a great many fellow sailors, that commercial vessels seldom respond to a call on the radio if you do not use the vessel's name. Radar cannot provide this and your call is likely to go unanswered unless it is a Mayday.
Remember though, that AIS only shows you the vessels that are transmitting and will not alert you to land masses, squalls or local fishermen!

HF Radio

With a far greater range than VHF, an HF radio can broadcast from just about anywhere on Earth and be heard by someone, somewhere. Many sailors form ad-hoc groups for a difficult passage and check in with one another each day at a given time to report their position and status. HF radios are also good for receiving weather reports and sending short emails (without attachments or pictures) via an additional piece of electronic gadgetry called a Pactor Modem. All this comes at a price of course. A system like this can cost you ten thousand dollars including installation (the backstay is used as an aerial, so there also has to be some changes to your rigging. You will also need a grounding aerial called a 'counterpoise'). A computer of some sort is needed to read the emails and weather reports. The whole system can be killed instantly by salt water or lightning and is notoriously fickle.

You will also need to sit a ridiculously complicated exam to license yourself and the radio itself will also require licensing.

If you don't fancy all that or fear that it may deal a killer blow to your bank account, but still need a way to access weather forecasts at sea, a little non-transmitting SSB radio of the type made by Sangean might be the answer. They are cheap, effective, do not require fitting or licensing and can be stored in a waterproof container when not in use. You will not be able to transmit any messages, but you will still be able to hear the weather forecast and any marine warnings. You will also be able to listen in on the nets of other sailors and glean much information in that way. I used mine to listen to the cricket during a gale and found it very comforting.

A transmitting HF radio is undoubtedly a good tool when it works, but certainly do not take the money from your hull, rigging or anchor budget to buy one. Remember: nothing electronic is as valuable as a strong boat.

Total Waste of Money Navigation Gear

Wind Speed Indicator

You do not really need a complicated gizmo to tell you the wind is picking up on a monohull boat. Firstly, you have your skin, ears and eyes. Secondly you have the boat itself, which will heel, speed up or become difficult to manage until you bring some sail down. If you have a wind generator, it will be generating more current and making more noise. Get used to estimating wind strength with your senses and you will become a better sailor.

Learn the Beaufort Scale and you should be able to guess the wind speed to within five or six knots. If you simply have to put an exact number to the wind speed, buy a hand-held anemometer, as the ones on the top of the mast are expensive, too vulnerable to bird landings and complicated to fit.

Wind Direction Indicator

Even more useless than a wind speed indicator. You can tell where the wind is coming from by feeling it on your face or looking at the sails or the spray. You certainly do not need to spend hundreds of dollars on a gizmo to see which way the wind is blowing! Why not do what we do on *Calypso*? A few days after buying her, we moved out of the marina where she was being kept, to the lovely anchorage nearby. Within a week, a pelican had landed on the electronic gizmo on top of the mast that senses and transmits the direction of the wind to a display at the helm. The replacement cost would have been $600 and would have lasted exactly as long as it would have taken another pelican to land on it.

Instead of diving head first into the murky world of yachting consumerism, we covered the screen with a particularly cool picture of Jimmy Cliff and tied a bit wool to the shrouds. This not only shows the wind direction more precisely than the electronic gizmo, it also provides a lot more information too:

If it is drooping, there is no wind.

If it is parallel to the boat, there is good wind.

If it is whipping and cracking, there is a LOT of wind.

If it is wet, it is raining.

If it has blown away, it might be time to heave-to.

I dare say that to some sailors at least, this system is not as sexy as a machine with fancy blinking lights, but it is cheaper and more accurate and does not break down. Spending your hard earned money on a device to tell you where the wind is coming from makes as much sense as buying a device to tell you if it is raining or when your wife is angry. If you can't tell on your own, then it is not unlikely or pessimistic in any way to expect a spot of bother in the very near future.

Chapter 16

Love Me Tender

If you think the same as everybody else around you it is fair to say that you are not so much a representative of your culture, but a victim of it.

Buddhist Proverb

Inflatable dinghies and ribs with big, powerful outboards are a great example of how some of the less desirable land-based values are becoming more common at sea. There are no more meetings to go to, the kids don't need picking up from school and traffic is never an issue. There is plenty of parking space and the beaches have endless availability. Time is no longer money and the joys the sailing life offers are not affected one bit by knocking a minute or two off the time it takes you to get ashore. Yet some sailors seem to find it difficult to shake their old land-based habits, and those that owned a BMW at home often bring the same attitude to sea.

Whilst writing this chapter, the World ARC (a big rally for cruisers) has arrived in Nuku Hiva. As soon as they had anchored their huge, flashy boats (the minimum requirement for the World ARC is 40 feet), they were flying ashore in their $20,000 dinghies spraying all around them, polluting the atmosphere and rolling yachts around with their wakes. (PLEASE! I am trying to make banana pancakes).

Why is it that having spent the last few weeks travelling 3000 miles at 6 miles an hour, they must finish the last 100 meters like Nikki Lauder? Fortunately, these folk being possessed of the very opposite of the sea gypsy ethos, cannot keep still and they will all be on their way tomorrow in their continuing quest for the 'miles under the keel' bragging rights that are such an important part of sailing for the spiritually challenged.

Despite its popularity, the inflatable dinghy/outboard combination is just about the worse choice a budget sailor can make as a tender for voyaging. They are expensive and delicate. They disintegrate in sunlight and rowing them is like trying to push a water bed through a vat of jam, hence the need for an outboard.

If you live in a calm anchorage, near a marina with a smooth dinghy dock and a repair shop, then the inflatable dinghy/outboard is okay I suppose. However, in the rest of the world, your expensive inflatable is going to be banging off oyster-encrusted wharfs or making difficult surf landings on rocky beaches. There are literally hundreds of wonderful anchorages where the dinghy/outboard combination simply cannot land due to the risk of overturning and killing the outboard forever. The owners often decide not to go ashore at all, or anchor off and swim through the surf (fine if you are having a beach day, not so great if you are taking your computer to the local internet spot or celebrating your anniversary in your finest threads and coiffure).

Furthermore, outboard motors are very tempting to thieves. The larger ones particularly are very much on the wish lists of fishermen all over the world (and are often worth the equivalent of a year's income to them). The thieves are rarely interested in the dinghy itself - these are often later found abandoned or slashed. The outboard is always the target. Many smart sea gypsies solve this problem by having a hard rowing tender. Unlike inflatables, a hard tender (fibreglass, plywood or polyethylene are popular) is virtually indestructible, undesirable to thieves and cheap to maintain.

Most people hate rowing because the only time they do it is when the outboard on their inflatable dinghy (invariably) breaks down. A proper rowing tender is a different bag of weevils entirely. Designed from the outset to be rowed, a decent hard tender glides easily through calm waters and happily bounces through rough chop like jelly on springs. It is fantastic for your figure and if you cock up your surf landing and flip it over (everybody does), you can stand up with a smile on your face, take a bow to anyone watching (there always is) and drag your little dinghy ashore with the only damage being your wounded pride (which, while it rarely feels like it at the time, is an easily renewable resource).

The owner of an overturned inflatable/outboard combo has to spring into immediate action if he is to save his drowned outboard before the salt water locks it up for good. Without a full strip down, many never recover.

Other Options

For the last year or so, Jasna and I have been looking at plans to build a sailing tender which will double as a life raft and have been collecting parts accordingly. The whole port side settee locker on *Calypso* contains mast, sails, rudder and rigging for our future hard, rowing/sailing/tender/liferaft. When we bought *Calypso* we inherited (as you probably will) an inflatable and an outboard. We have always hated them, but we thought to ourselves,

"Well, it's not worth much, so we will use it until it wears out and then get a proper rowing tender"

Big mistake.

We spent the next year, patching, repairing, servicing, patching, repairing, servicing – generating bills and frustration because we were in a place where we could not find a decent hard, rowing tender. We got around the problem by buying an Advanced Elements double kayak and have not regretted it. These make extremely dry and stable tenders for yachts, are fun to paddle and good for fitness. They slip through the water like underfed sharks, are stable and can carry amazing amounts to stuff. Although they are inflatable (and therefore still vulnerable to oyster encrusted docks) they are light and can be lifted out anywhere by one person. So when we come to a rough dock wall, we simply haul her out and let all the expensive dinghies bash against the quay while our lovely kayak sits under the shade of a tree. (see picture overleaf).

Surf landings are a cinch too. Once you get the hang of it, you can time your surf landing to allow you to glide in gracefully pretty much most of the time. Sure, we still get it wrong sometimes, but far less than the inflatable owner and with zero repercussions. With a couple of spare t-shirts in a dry-bag, we just take our bow and off we go again. No harm done.

Furthermore, when we go on passage, we can break the whole thing down (it has an aluminium backbone) and put it below – leaving our decks wonderfully clear to sail *Calypso* and not worry every time a wave strafes the foredeck.
Our Advanced Elements kayak has been on active duty as a main tender for 6 years and is now beginning to show her age. We have ordered another one and we are picking her up in Tahiti. You can learn more about Advanced Elements on our

website or on www.advancedelements.com (Don't forget to check us out on the ambassadors' page!).

Spiritual Issues

The environmental implications of outboards (particularly the huge ones that are becoming depressingly common) are obvious, but there are other, spiritual issues too.
Inflatable dinghies are not particularly hydrodynamic – they are not designed to slip through the water, but to be large and stable. Rowing one will not offer you anything like the rewards that gliding along in a proper rowing boat will. (If for some reason you are unable to row and must have an outboard, the good news is that a properly designed rowing tender will happily potter along with a cheap, green, 2hp unit).

The moment I sit in our kayak, I am a happy man. I can feel how she is designed to work with the water, how the waves break easily around her as she slips along with the slightest effort. Although she is low to the water, she is drier than an inflatable dinghy whose chubby love-handles slam into the smallest chop and send spray everywhere. Sitting in a tender that is designed from the outset to move through water is a beautiful feeling and that is why we came is it not?

Furthermore, I see much more marine life in my silent kayak. I can paddle up to huge manta rays, even whale sharks without scaring them off. I can hear the wind in the palm trees and the drums ashore. I can explore shallow rivers and coral reefs without worrying about my propeller or ruining the experience by drowning out the sounds of nature with the endless rattle of an engine. What price do I have to pay for this? Nothing. And I get a little, well-needed exercise thrown in for free.

But perhaps the biggest spiritual reward of rowing is slowing down. Not just for your own blood pressure, but for the marine life too. Traveling at more than 5 knots with an outboard motor does not give sea turtles enough time to get out of your way. A concerned environmentalist approached us in Mexico with a petition and information on the effects of fast dinghies on turtles and dolphins. The pictures were appalling – turtles with split shells, dolphins with half the dorsal fin missing. Figures are hard to find because most dolphins and turtles injured by propellers simply drift out to sea and are lost. However, a study in Georgia USA recently found that 20% of sea turtles had some propeller damage on their shells – and these are the ones that survived. The actual figures are almost certainly significantly higher. Either way, it is easy to see that flying around in a massive rib, mashing turtles and dolphins might be an unfair way to cope with a mid-life crisis.

If you have the resources, get rid of your outboard/inflatable dinghy combo as soon as you can. If you hang on to it and go sailing, it will almost certainly spit the dummy exactly where you can't find a decent hard tender (oh, sweetly doth speak the voice of experience). Sell it while it is still in reasonable condition and you may even make a small profit, as hard rowing tenders are cheaper than inflatable/outboard combos! If you are considering long sea journeys, try and find a tender that fits behind the mast as it will be more secure there and on no account fit davits, unless you never intend to go offshore (see chapter 4).

If you are bit pressed for space, there are some great designs for nesting tenders (tenders that split in two and store on top of one another like Russian dolls). Why not build one as part of educating yourself in boat repair? To see the one we are building, see bandbyachtdesigns.com.

At the very least, if you simply must have an inflatable/outboard combo, get a small one with a small, environmentally friendly engine and try and keep in mind that we share the anchorages with other creatures – most of whom have been here a lot longer than us and have done nothing to deserve our contempt.[11]

---

[11] The amount of humans injured or killed by fast tenders is also on the rise. Snorkelers are particularly vulnerable, as is anyone out and about at night. All outboards are fitted with a 'kill switch' which can be attached to the operator and stops the engine when he falls overboard. In all our time afloat, we have never seen anyone use them. There is really no reason for this as it only takes a second to wrap it around your ankle. Always use yours, not just for your own sake, but for those who will have to deal with your out of control, over-powered dinghy when you fall overboard. Special mention has to go to the young American cruiser John from S/V *Time Piece* who lost a leg recently in La Paz, while rescuing another sailor from such a situation. John is a hero, no doubt, but his is just one accident that could have been easily prevented by using the 'kill switch'

Chapter 17

Stayin' Alive

The best safety equipment you can have is a good strong boat of the type we have been advocating throughout this book and the right attitude and skills to use it safely.

The yachting community is a strange beast. We personally know at least two boats that have needed mid-ocean rescue because their unprotected spade rudder hit a submerged object and ripped a hole in their hull. They set off their EPIRB (an electronic beacon that sends a distress signal and position) and jumped in their life raft. They were fortunate enough to be rescued.

So what does the yachting community conclude from this? That it is insane to go to sea without a life raft and an EPIRB. You can see where I am going with this. Tell someone that you have no life raft or EPIRB and they will throw up their hands in utter horror while setting sail in their flashy yoghurt-pot with its unprotected rudder and badly attached keel whilst simultaneously boasting how fast she is. In fact every time another yachtsman gets into trouble by ignoring good seamanship and seaworthy yacht design, the press is full of stories of how their safety gear saved their bacon, rather than looking at why the safety gear was needed in the first place

When a boat loses its keel, hits a well-charted reef, or has its unprotected rudder smashed to bits by a log, it is far better for the sailor bent on mitigation to ask a different set of questions.

If you have read this far, I bet you can guess fairly accurately what those questions might be.

After the ill-fated Sydney-Hobart race of 1998 it seemed everyone was discussing which safety gear worked best and which was found lacking. This happens pretty much every time there is a mass race tragedy and gets a lot of press – particularly if a certain type of life raft worked badly or an EPIRB failed to send a signal. New standards for safety equipment are set, everything becomes more expensive and manufacturers add another wing to their converted water mill in Tuscany.

Far more interesting from the viewpoint of a responsible skipper (or anyone who really wants to understand risk) is which boat designs, tactics and attitudes resulted in the least amount of safety gear needing deployment in the first place, but these are seldom mentioned. Similarly ignored were the 66 captains who decided to turn back to Sydney and not risk the lives of their crew.

These wily captains hardly ever merit a mention. Not because they weren't good skippers (which they clearly were, as the difficult decision they made not carry on turned out to be the right one) but because they were not newsworthy skippers. The skippers that received all the attention were those 'courageous' captains that, in the search for glory, ignored their first responsibility (which - legally and morally - is the safety of all onboard) and put their crew's lives at risk by heading out in atrocious conditions and then calling upon others to risk their lives in order to rescue them.

Now, don't get me wrong here. I am not even remotely saying that safety gear is superfluous. What I am saying is that preventing accidents by getting real about the risks you really face, leaving your land-based ideas on land, respecting the sea and ditching any ridiculous ideas of goal setting and trophy-lifting, is not just better than cure - it is a million times better than cure. The sailor with the right boat and attitude, but no life raft is many times safer than the sailor with the wrong boat, wrong attitude and the best life raft money can buy.

Are there cases when a good sea boat needs a life raft? Yes, of course (a fire on board in fairly benign conditions for example), but choosing an un-seaworthy boat, strapping a life raft to it and heading out in crazy conditions is like relying on abortion as birth control – there is so much you can do to avoid it (including total abstinence when conditions are most risky).

Getting real, seeing through the hype of 'go-getting' mentality, choosing the right boat that is properly designed for the sea and developing good, defensive seamanship - these are the pre-requisites of a safe life afloat. Life rafts, EPIRBs, satellite phones, etc, are all extra little trinkets that you can add to your good preparations – not a substitute for them. So let's have a look at some of the more commonly used bits of safety gear. We may as well start with inflatable life rafts, seeing as how I have been banging on about them for a while now.

The Inflatable Life Raft.

Inflatable life rafts are flimsy, temperamental sheets of PVC that rely on complicated gas systems to inflate them and hydrostatic (responding to water pressure) devices to release them. Because of the expense involved in re-packing them, it is unlikely that you will get any practice deploying yours at all. Nor can you test them. I could wax on for pages about the importance of 'drill' in emergency situations, but the point I most want to make about inflatable life rafts is this:

Many people think a thin, complicated PVC vessel will survive in conditions severe enough to sink their yacht because it has the word 'life' in the title. In other words, because it says so on the packet.

There are plenty of stories of sailors whose lives were saved by a life raft that confirm this view. We seldom hear reports from sailors whose life rafts failed to inflate or broke up instantly - probably for the very good reason that these lost souls are living with the mermaids. Unhappy customers seldom return, making an accurate survey of the benefits of life rafts almost impossibly one-sided.

There is good reason to suspect that the increase in confidence in inflatable life rafts over the years is related to the decreasing inclusion of seaworthiness as an essential part of yacht design. Imagine a storm that could destroy *Calypso* (or any other heavily-built sea boat with an integral keel and a defensive crew that knows how to heave-to). There is no way that abandoning into a PVC life raft in those kind of conditions is going to do anything other than delay your death for a few minutes. However, as yacht designs become less seaworthy, the likelihood of having to abandon your boat in fairly benign conditions increases. Thin fin keels fall off (more than once in the case of some boats like the Bavaria Match 42 or the Beneteau First 40.7), unprotected spade rudders crowbar fatal holes in the hull upon collision with floating debris and increasingly competitive mentality leads to bad decision making (too many cases to mention here. See chapter 8) – all in fairly benign conditions that would not have worried *Calypso* or any good sea-boat crewed by defensive sailors.

The lack of seaworthiness in yacht design does not prove the value of PVC life rafts, but does increase their use in benign conditions and therefore the amount of good reports regarding their essential nature.

An increasingly popular alternative to the inflatable life raft is the hard sailing tender that converts to a life raft.
You can either beef up your existing sailing tender or buy a sailing tender that is designed to double as a life raft of the type made by Portland (www.portland.com).

The Portland is a little expensive for most budget sailors, but considering they are an indestructible tender, a fun sailing toy and tough sailing life raft (that does not need expensive yearly servicing) all rolled into one, it is worth keeping an eye out for a used one.

Whether you splash out for a Portland or modify your existing hard sailing tender, this type of life raft/tender system has several distinct advantages over the inflatable.

Firstly, it is more economical and a great deal more fun to convert your hard tender into a sailing life raft than to simply buy an inflatable life raft that needs expensive yearly servicing.

Secondly, it is more economical in terms of space as you will not have to find room for both a tender and a life raft on your small boat.

Thirdly (and perhaps most importantly) this system allows the operator to build confidence through practice and regular use. The importance of 'drill' in disaster situations has been established beyond doubt and the couple who practice abandoning into their life raft has a very significant advantage of those who hope to wing it. The sailing life raft also offers the crew the chance to save themselves by making some progress towards land - rather than lolling about passively waiting to be rescued in an orange bouncy castle full of puke.

In the more remote parts of the world, making your own way towards land may be your only hope of survival anyway, so some kind of propulsion would seem a sensible idea and the wind is the obvious choice.

Grab Bag

So you have jumped in your life raft and are feeling pretty pleased with yourselves for having such a great thing on board. If you don't have supplies, then all you have probably done is extend your suffering a little longer until the hand of death caresses your cheek in merciful release.

If you have a nice sailing life raft, you can store your supplies permanently in the flotation chambers and inspect them regularly. If you have an inflatable, there are a few supplies inside it, but you will need more, so a grab bag is required. A grab bag should be brightly coloured, preferably buoyant and contain all your survival stuff in one neat package. Here is what is in ours:

EPIRB (see below)

Compass

Manual, pump-action watermaker

Solar Still

Signalling mirror

Waterproof VHF radio

Waterproof GPS

A gazillion batteries in waterproof bag

Pencils and Paper in a waterproof bag

Pacific Chart

Passports

$500

Fishing gear

Flares

Sea sickness tablets

2 x plastic miniatures of rum to toast the passing of *Calypso*

We also have a secondary grab bag that contains tins of food. We keep a second bag because it does not pay to make your primary grab bag too heavy. On top of all this, we keep six, 20 litre jerry cans of water lashed to the deck. The jerry cans are only 75% full, to ensure that they are sufficiently buoyant.

EPIRBs

An EPIRB (pronounced 'ee-perb') is a little beacon that can transmit your position in an emergency. When everything has gone wrong and you are sitting in your life raft in your underwear with a stupid look on your face, this might be your last chance of a rescue. Owning an EPIRB is particularly important if you have a life raft that cannot make progress towards land. When they first came out, the cost was a bit of an issue, but now they have become relatively affordable, we always have one. Get the one that can have its batteries changed by the operator and you will have few maintenance costs.

Iridium Phones

Seem to work well, but are way too expensive to operate for the average sea gypsy. Anyway, I rather like not being on the phone. I don't even own a mobile.

HF Radios

With an HF radio you can talk to people around the world and receive weather information and short emails (too slow for any attachments or pictures). The initial set-up costs are high, but the running costs (even email) are free from then on. There is no doubt that HF radios have saved a few lives and if your boat has one, you would do well to learn to use it.

Radar (see Chapter 15)

Radar Reflector

Whether you have your own radar or not, there is really no excuse not to have a radar reflector up your mast so that you can be easily seen on the radar of other boats. Sailboats have a very small radar signature, but by installing a $20 radar reflector up your mast, you make a much bigger impression on the screens of approaching super tankers. (Jasna made ours by stuffing a PVC tube full of aluminium foil and mounting it up the mast. Our friends say we show up like the USS *Nimitz* on the radar).

Staying on Board

I am not going to join the already bloodied arena of the life jacket debate. Figures show that your chances of survival increase dramatically if you are wearing one. The US Coast Guard report of 2012 shows that of the 459 people who drowned that year, only 71 were wearing life jackets.[12]

However, most boating accidents happen fairly close to shore (where most people use their boats) and this is where those figures are compiled. The truth is a little different offshore. When sailing offshore, it is best to concentrate your efforts on staying on board. Do not look at the water as a beautiful blue ocean. Imagine instead that it is molten lava. It might as well be, because you are as good as dead if you fall overboard, particularly at night. Rig jack lines and stay clipped on – a good harness will serve you better than a good life jacket.

---

[12] United States Coast Guard Report on Recreational Boating Statistics 2012. Commandant Publication P16754.26

A good middle way is to buy a fairly non-intrusive life jacket that has a harness built into it. If you happen to fall overboard while coastal sailing, the jacket will help you stay afloat while you wait to be rescued, so they are not a total waste of time. As fairly good swimmers, we prefer the manual inflating type, as our first line of defence is to swim towards the boat and we don't want an automatically inflated life jacket spoiling our stroke.

Man Overboard and Self-Steering

Whether you are sailing as part of a small crew or single-handing, you will often be on watch alone. If you fall overboard whilst steering by hand, your boat would probably round up (turn into the wind) and stop, at least giving you a chance to get back on board. However, the chances are that for much of your lone watch, your wind vane or autopilot will be taking care of the steering and should you fall overboard in these conditions, you will have to suffer the added insult of watching your perfectly trimmed boat sail off into the distance as you tread water waiting for the Kraken to pull you down to Davy Jones with its fiery suckers. So particular attention has to be paid by the lone watchman when self-steering is operating.

To help mitigate this risk on *Calypso* we have introduced two practices when alone on watch.

1. Nobody ever leaves the cockpit alone for any reason whatsoever.

If there is a problem on deck, Jasna MUST wake me. I am not required to help solve the problem (there are few tasks on *Calypso* that cannot be performed solo), just to sit in the cockpit half asleep and drooling while she sorts out whatever needs doing. When she returns, I grunt and go back down below and continue to snore in a way that only a mother could love. This may sound inconvenient, but as we always reef down at night anyway, it does not happen too frequently.

2. We trail a long floating line behind the boat

This is not so the condemned person can partake in a little water skiing before entering Davy Jones' Locker (not a bad idea though). This line is attached to the self-steering control line and releases it from its cam-cleat when tugged hard. If I fall overboard, I will swim like Nemo to this line, pull it and cling on like a barnacle. *Calypso* will round up nicely (which will wake Jasna by tossing her out of bed) and I get a second chance. (This is another good reason to slow down at night – it is fairly difficult to hang on to a line at high speed and absolutely impossible if your life jacket has auto-inflated).

The above are just a few ideas of what you can you do to improve safety in your new life, but I want to end this chapter the same way as I started it:

The best safety equipment you can have is a good strong boat of the type we have been describing throughout this book and the right attitude and skills to use it safely.

The US Coast Guard report quoted earlier also points out that the single biggest contributing factor to boating deaths is alcohol. Alcohol accounted for at least twice as many deaths as any other contributing factor including bad weather, hazardous conditions, operator inattention, operator inexperience or big waves. If there was a company manufacturing a product that had as positive an effect on boating safety as good old sober abstinence, I guarantee you would be seeing it in all the yachting press with the tag-line "don't leave port without it."

Do not underestimate the value of the right attitude simply because nobody has found a way of making a fortune marketing it.

Chapter 18

A Brief Word About Rigging

There is no doubt that good rigging is essential to your safety. Rigging is expensive, but only a fool ignores it. However, there are many things you can do to mitigate the expense of a new rig. Firstly, do as much of it yourself as possible. Rigging takes a bit of thinking about, but it is not rocket science and with the introduction of mechanical terminals (such as Norseman, Sta-lock and Hayn), it is no longer essential to have huge hydraulic presses to make swages – just a vice and a couple of wrenches.

Secondly, find somebody else who is planning on re-rigging their boat and approach a rigging supplier together. Many rigging suppliers allow you to open a trade account if you order more than a certain amount of stuff and I have found their requirements are fairly relaxed. This can save you nearly half the cost right there.

On many occasions, it may not be necessary to change the entire rig. The great French circumnavigator Bernard Moitessier would replace the lower terminals more often as these are the ones that suffer the most from being constantly doused in salt water. Corrosion happens much more quickly at deck level than up the mast where the terminals are largely spared the salt water hosing and are also upside down and therefore, less likely to fill with water.
Moitessier would simply cut the wires above the corrosion point, and make up the difference with a piece of stainless

chain. Confused? Take a look at the diagram below:

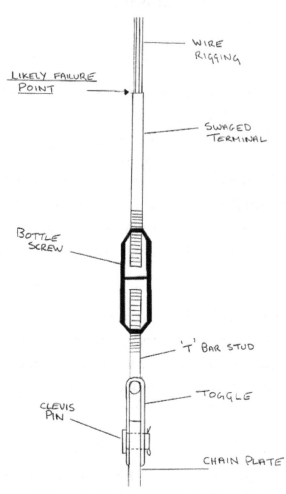

The lower part of your rigging probably looks something like this. If the toggle, bottle screw or any other parts need replacing, they are pretty straight forward to fit. However, one of the most common failures is at the point where the stainless wire enters the swage (as shown on the diagram). These tend to corrode due to the constant barrage of seawater infiltrating the swage. Eventually, the individual wires start to break at the point they enter the swage (these broken wires are often referred to as "meat hooks" due to their ability to make your hands look like a kebab). As soon as you see one meat hook, or any cracks or deformity, it is already well past time to do something about it. This is much more difficult to repair than simply replacing a toggle or bottle screw. Many choose to replace the entire strand and if you can afford it, this is the way to go. If you are flat broke or in the middle of nowhere, you need to get creative. Here is what Moitessier would do.

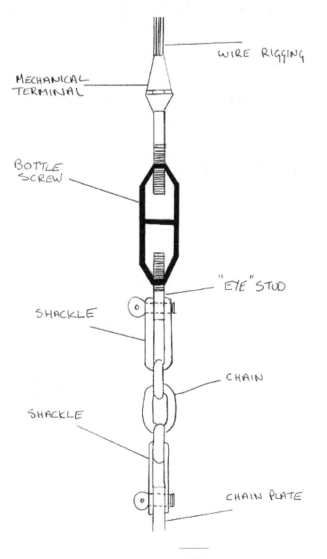

Moitessier would cut off the corroded end of the wire rigging and replace the swage with a mechanical terminal further up the wire where there was no corrosion (in the interest of historical accuracy, what Moitessier did was form a thimbled loop with saddle clamps because mechanical terminals were not available then).

This of course would mean that the rigging wire was shorter than before and no longer reached the deck, so he would then make up the difference with a short length of chain and *voila* – a simple, quick and economical repair that has avoided the need to junk the whole line. While it is always preferable to change the whole strand if you can, for reasons of location, emergency or general poverty, this is not always possible and Moitessier's method is certainly a big improvement on a dodgy lower swage. The added length of chain actually adds a bit of twist capability, which can help the wire absorb some of the strain and reduce work hardening.

Moitessier used this method his whole sailing career and I believe his famous boat *Joshua* had the same actual wire (with ever-lengthening pieces of chain) for much longer than is currently vogue without any problems. *Joshua* was eventually wrecked off Cabo San Lucas, but not due to rigging failure. Obviously, if you have a problem aloft, the same technique is valid, but the upper terminals tend to outlast the lowers by a significant margin, so it is likely that you would only need to concentrate on the lowers. If, however there was a problem aloft, I would still be tempted to add the chain at deck level, where it is less likely to come into contact with the sails and can be easily covered where it might. Bernard Moitessier may not have been everybody's cup of tea, but 50,000 sea miles, solo in one go definitely qualifies as "testing in the big tank". If you do the right thing and get a whole new strand, you can increase the life of your new rigging by flipping it end-to-end every couple of years. This not only helps you avoid the above predicament of lower swage corrosion, but also helps change the geography of the stress points in the strand and hence avoid the concentrations of repetitive stresses that lead to work hardening and failure.

Now if all that seems like a highly confusing mountain of hassle and you are already starting to think that Facebook might be more fun, don't sweat it too much – it is much easier to understand when it is in front of you. However, if you find the whole subject of rigging about as interesting as a hermit's diary, then you definitely need to go back to chapter 5 and have a closer look at the junk rig which avoids the whole tin of worms by using un-rigged, free-standing masts. You can then rip out this chapter and throw it overboard with all your rigging spares and use the extra space to store the huge pile of cash you are going to save.

Chapter 19

Staying Healthy - Budget Provisioning

(or The Lesser of Two Weevils)

If you follow our advice and stay away from marinas, marine professionals and expensive gear you don't need, your main expense should be food (in fact this is a good way to know you have got it right. If you have any bills larger than food,

then that is the area that needs addressing). Therefore, the way you do your provisioning can have a huge impact on your budget. But before I get into details, I want to assure you that eating on a budget doesn't mean eating badly.

I (Jasna) was born in Italy. Everybody knows Italian cuisine and most people love it. But Italian food is one of the simplest in the world. It is true what my Mamma always says:

"The secret of Italian food is not in the ingredients, but in the creativity."

A long time ago in Naples, a cook wanted to make a special dish in honour of Queen Margherita. He looked around the kitchen and found only flour, cheese, tomatoes and some spices. Not much. But he was a creative man and not easily discouraged. That was the day the pizza was born (the basic pizza is still called the 'margherita').

The same goes for your galley. Be creative. If you have flour, oil, cheese, tomatoes and eggs, you can have bread, bruschettas, focaccias, tortillas, pancakes, biscuits, quiches, pizzas and cakes. Then you only need some fresh fruit or vegetables to spice things up; garlic bread, banana pancakes, carrot cake, pizza with mushrooms, spinach and cheese crepes, breaded aubergines, veggie burgers, mushroom quiche. Add a few beans and lentils and the world is your pearl-laden oyster – even before we get on to meat and fish.

Our adjusted accounts clearly show that our food costs are three times higher when we are next to a town than when we are anchored on a deserted island. This is because the shops make you lazy. It is easier to buy bread, camembert and ham instead of making a pizza. It is easier to buy a fruit juice than squeeze a handful of oranges. It is easier to buy soy burgers than to make them, but it costs *fifty* times more. It is much easier to buy cheese, yoghurt or ketchup than to make it yourself.

I cannot recommend highly enough the book *Sailing the Farm* by Ken Neumeyer, which is full of great ideas and recipes for sea gypsies living on a budget (see appendix). This book really helps me keep our budget on track. Amongst other things, this book shows how to make cheese and yoghurt, which seaweed is edible, how to preserve fish without a fridge and how to sprout different seeds.

These are all useful skills, but the main secret to cheap provisioning is to eat the way the locals do. In Mexico we lived on tortillas, which cost $1 per kilo, while a baguette cost $3 and was mainly air. In Tahiti, where 1kg of tortillas cost an astonishing $20, we lived on baguettes, which cost 50 cents. If something we love in one area is too expensive in another, we simply learn to live without it and find something else to like.

Remember: Part of getting real is understanding that the human mind can be changed in an instant, while flying your favourite brand of peanut butter all the way from California is expensive, problematic, environmentally disastrous and a good sign that you still have a way to go. It is easy to change your mind about what you want if you are adventurous and not hung up on your right to immediate gratification. Not only will you save money, you will also discover many new tastes. (The spiritual benefits of this approach could fill another book).

One of the main staples in Europe and America is the potato. In the Marquesas Islands they are imported, expensive and not very fresh. Rather than stamp your feet and throw teddy out of the pram, why not try the interesting looking, locally grown sweet potatoes? Admittedly purple is a strange colour for a spud, but if you squeeze lemon on them they become bright pink! So if you don't fixate on having your imagined desires instantly gratified, you will not only discover a wonderful new taste, but also be able to write messages or draw pink pictures on your psychedelic purple mash during lunch. Now, what is not to like about that? And all it costs is the milliamp of electricity it takes to change a thought.

A bag of 6 apples in French Polynesia costs $10, while grapefruit, mangoes and bananas are almost free. We love apples and (in other parts of the world) practically live off them on passages. Now we live on bananas. There are some islands where fruits are plentiful and cheap, while others where nothing grows. This is why you have to plan ahead. Get the fruit while it is free and stow it away. There are many ways of conserving it. I choose drying because it is fast, simple and safe. Dried fruit is a delicious healthy snack in its own right, but you can also soak dried fruit overnight and use it to make fruit smoothies, yoghurts or pies.

The dryer can also be used to dry vegetables (dried tomatoes are fantastic!), fish and meat. I also use it to make my very own fruit bars. This is a great way of saving those last six overripe bananas that have started to look pretty sad because nobody wants to eat them. I mash or blend the fruit with the juice of one small lime, add some honey, a cup of rolled oats, sesame seeds, nuts and whatever else I find in the cupboard. Then I spread this thick sauce onto a sheet of grease-proof paper and put it in the dryer. After two days, I flip the semi-dried sauce over and peel the paper off. Another two days in the sun and the bars are ready to be cut and stowed away. These cheap, healthy and super energetic fruit bars can really change your mood during a long, wet night watch.

It is not hard to make your own dryer, but given the price of the commercially available ones, I didn't bother. This is the one we use and are very happy with it. They soon pay for themselves. Get two and use one for fish only, as there is nothing quite as bad as fish flavour permeating other foods. The only thing that should taste of fish is fish. (More about the food dryer on our website)

It is important to know how to preserve the provisions you buy and you will need a few tricks up your sleeve. It makes sense to stock up where provisions are cheap, but there is absolutely no point in doing this if the tins get rusty, the eggs go bad, the pasta and flour become a weevil farm and most of the fruit rots.

If you have a fridge, it is a little bit easier, but you should still know how to survive without it, because marine fridges break down all the time and are usually too small to store very much anyway.

If you have a freezer, sell it at the next boat jumble. Don't get me wrong; I would love to have a freezer. And in fact, we know many people that have one and swear by it. But these people don't live on a budget. For a budget sailor the implications of a freezer are rather onerous. To power a freezer, you will need more solar panels which means a bigger solar controller and thicker wiring to handle the increased load and more batteries to store the power needed overnight. You will almost certainly have to start your engine or buy a generator to keep your batteries topped up (particularly on cloudy days), which means more fuel, bigger tanks and so on. When any part of the system inevitably breaks down, you will have a large repair bill to contemplate whilst throwing a lot of expensive food overboard. Forget about it and use that money to buy yourself an ice cream every time you go shopping.

Important rules about keeping food aboard:

- Never bring cardboard onto the boat unless you feel lonely and want to have a colony of cockroaches to keep you company.

- Move as much stuff as you can to plastic containers to minimize the rubbish and keep the insects from spreading bag to bag.

- Eggs and vegetables are easy to keep fresh without a fridge as long as you make sure that they have never been previously refrigerated. In Australia I used to keep carrots for months without a fridge by wrapping them tightly in newspaper. Here in the Polynesian islands, the carrots arrive frozen from Tahiti and they rarely last more than two days.

- It is a good idea to wash fruits and vegetables (except lettuces which tend to rot) in a weak solution of bleach and water when you bring them aboard to kill the bacteria and get rid of unwanted guests. Be especially careful with bananas and pineapples because they can store an incredible amount of ugly insects. We always submerge the whole stand of bananas in the sea for a minute before bringing it aboard. Once a gecko floated away and we felt so bad that Rick jumped in the kayak and rescued him with a colander. He became Gordon, our first pet. Gordon had a happy life keeping *Calypso* free of insects, scoffing bananas and generally popping up unexpectedly.

- Eggs can last up to two months without refrigeration if you remember to turn them over every few days. If you are going on a long passage you can coat them with Vaseline and they will last even longer. It is a good idea to have a plastic egg-holder because in many countries eggs are sold loose. The problem with these containers is that in the tropics the eggs can get mouldy. We solved this problem by drilling a few holes in each compartment.

- Don't overbuy things that you can easily find anywhere. Even the smallest village shop will usually have some flour, so it makes little sense buying huge 20kg bags unless you are planning to winter in the Arctic circle. Be aware that storing flour is not as easy as it sounds. If the bag breaks you will have a big clean up job to do, and if it gets wet you will end up with a bilge full of... oh what does flour and water make again? Oh yeah. Glue. A better way to store flour is in a sealed plastic container with a small piece of cotton wool that has been soaked in alcohol. The fumes will kill any insect eggs and your flour will be weevil-free.

- Write the contents on the top of every tin. Some people even peel the labels off to avoid insect eggs and varnish them to keep them from rusting. I have never found the need for it, but if you plan to keep the tins in the bilge it is probably a good idea as seawater ingress will loosen the labels and clog the bilge pumps just at the moment you need them to work.

- If you find something rare at a good price with a good shelf life, buy mountains of it! We left Mexico with 40 bags of corn tortillas and they got demolished quicker than England's World Cup dreams.

- It is a good idea to write down where you put stuff. I occasionally forget to do it and have often paid the price. Once I found a forgotten bag of apples that had been tucked under the spare lifejackets for seven months. You don't want to know the details, but I still have nightmares and will probably never own an iPad.

- We don't eat much meat, but fish is an important part of our diet. We often catch tuna or dorado while trolling on passage and we also like to spear-fish. If we catch too much we share it with our neighbours in the anchorage. This is a great way of making new friends. Cut your spare fish into fillets, drop a couple into a zip-lock bag and hop in the kayak - instant chums and good karma too. If you still have too much fish, it can be made to last several days longer by putting it in a pickling solution of half water and half vinegar. Whatever is left can be sliced, salted and put in the drier. Vacuum packing is an option for the budget cruiser as small inexpensive kits are now readily available. We currently have one on order and will report on our website whether they are as good as they look.

To be a successful fisherman you should talk to the locals. They will tell you where and when to fish and which are the best lures to use in their waters. Another great source of information is *The Cruisers Handbook of Fishing* by Scott and Wendy Bannerot. If you intend to fish to eat (rather than for pleasure or competition) this is the only book you will need (see appendix).

Another word about local people: when you provision, think about them too. On many islands the shops have a very poor choice. Whereas, you may have just arrived from Panama, (or any other land of cheap provisioning) stuffed to the gunwales with interesting goods. If you have space on your boat, it pays to find out what people are short of in the next country you are planning to visit. Buy heaps, take it ashore and swap it for fruit or services. You will get a good deal and the locals will love you! In the atoll of Toau, we paid our mooring fees with three tins of fruit and a few cartons of Mexican cream. We saved $100 and the owner was so happy she didn't stop hugging me. Be careful where you get your information though - we were told that people in the Marquesas desperately needed reading glasses. We bought 50 pairs in Mexico and still have all of them.

One other thing that has a big impact on the cost of provisioning is drinks of all sorts. Learn to love home-made beverages: lemonade, iced tea - we even make our own wine aboard. A bottle of cheap rum goes a long way because it can be added to coconut, mango, papaya or whatever fruit you can find to make cheap, delicious cocktails. On our previous boat we had a little microbrewery for our own beer. Develop a taste for these, rather than doggedly sticking to your old preferences, and every month you will save enough for a rent-a-car adventure around the island.

As we have seen elsewhere in this book, moving from land to sea requires a change of attitude. Trying to copy/paste your old life into this new environment will lead you into the ultimately unsatisfying world of consumer yachting as you try to satisfy your land-based tastes with freezers, gelato machines, coffee percolators, imported foods, ice-makers, microwaves and all the other 'essentials' that absolutely nobody had, on land or sea, 50 years ago and which cause nothing but trouble at sea. It is both easier and ultimately more rewarding to leave your land-based habits on land and embrace this wonderful new life you have chosen.

Learning how to fish, cook, bake and dry food shouldn't be an irksome task but a pleasure. In our busy city lives we rarely bake a loaf of bread or sprout a radish seed simply because we don't have the time. Once you move to the sea you will be 'time rich'.

This is a great opportunity to rediscover the joys of using simple foods to produce wholesome meals, of kneading bread in the early morning, squeezing exotic fruits under a tropical sun, and to divest ourselves of the constant consumer chatter that pushes us to further complicate our lives with ridiculous gadgets and soul-free convenience foods. In no time at all you will rediscover the joys of slow cooking and be able to condemn frozen meals, sliced bread and microwaveable pizza to the dustbin where in reality, they have always belonged.

Chapter 20

To insure or not to insure?

For the wealthy yachtsman, this is easy to answer. If you have a million dollar yacht then what is another $15,000 for insurance? For us sea gypsies living on a limited budget, a little more thought has to go into our decision.

Living without insurance

I know plenty of budget sailors and sea gypsies who have insurance and plenty who do not. Of those that do not, many 'self-insure'. To self-insure, you take the premium you would have paid to the insurance company and place it in a long-term, high-interest deposit account. You do this every year. If your boat gets hit by lightning and you need to replace your electrics, then you access the money. If (like the majority of people) you never need to make a 'claim' on your money, then the deposit account keeps growing and eventually you get the premiums back when your sailing days are over.

The weakness in the above system is that you might sink the boat the day after you buy it, before you have had time to accumulate any real funds. The strength of this system is that your precious resources are not swallowed up to provide skiing holidays for insurance brokers and you get to keep the premiums if you don't claim. Of course, there will always be accidents, but as you have followed the advice in this book and bought a strong sea-boat, taken the time to get to know her, divested yourself of competitive thinking and generally gotten real about the risks, then you are far less likely to be in one. Because you have bought a modest boat, you are also much more capable of bouncing back from a total loss than the sailor who has sold his home and/or taken a huge loan to fund his 70ft floating ego. If the worst comes to the worst and you have to replace your modest, uninsured boat, the chances are you may have to replace it with something even more modest. If you have the right outlook and have become accustomed to the joys of living frugally, you may even enjoy the enforced simplicity of the replacement more than your original boat. The rich yachtsman replacing his 70ft floating ego with a 60ft floating ego will always see it as a loss.

Insure v Self Insure – a Comparison.

Let's look at the case of our friend Ignacio who bought a good little sea boat to fix up for $20,000. After a very relaxed couple of years and another $6000, he had her up and running and decided to anchor in the lovely bay of La Cruz on the Mexican Riviera.

Unfortunately, Ignacio decided to use rope rather than chain to anchor (a questionable technique often used by competitive sailors to lighten the weight in the bow and therefore increase speed). Pretty soon, the rope had chafed through on an underwater rock and his boat was lying on the reef by the little town of Huanacaxtle, damaged beyond repair. Ignacio pitched a tent (to stop looters), stripped the boat of everything he could and held a garage sale on the beach (we still have some of his rigging).

Let's have a look at how the figures add up if he were insured or decided to self-insure.

Self Insured

Two years of premiums @ $800 placed in a deposit account @ 5% interest means he has $1682 in his self insurance fund
Receipts from beach sale = $7400
Total loss = cost of boat − receipts from beach sale
Total loss equals $26000 -$7400

Total Loss = $18,600 (but Ignacio still has $1682 he has saved in his self insurance fund to get going again)

Insured

The agreed value for insurance purposes will normally be the value of the boat and a percentage of the improvements. It is rare that you can insure for the full value of your improvements, so despite the total coast of the boat being $26,000, the insured value is more likely to have been nearer $22,500. So:

Total sum insured = $22,500
Less $1500 (the value of the dinghy/outboard which was ashore with Ignacio at the time)
Less $7400 (yes, any value salvaged from the wreck will be deducted from the payout)
Less excess @ 1500
Likely payout = $12,100
Remember to subtract $1682 (the two years of premiums and lost interest on the money) and what you are really getting is: $10,418
Total Loss = $26000 – $10,418

Total loss = $15,582

In Ignacio's case, the difference between the two systems is only $3000 and change.

Ignoring for now that the insurance company would probably claim (with some justification) that the owner was negligent for not using good anchor chain and refuse to pay out a penny anyway, you can see that it does not take too many years of self-insurance before you are in the money. Do the sum again after a longer period and the figures begin to close and eventually swap places. Of course if you don't wreck your boat (which will be the story for the overwhelming majority) then, the self-insurer wins by a country mile. If your boat sinks without a trace the day after you launch it, the insured boat wins.

Living with insurance

Those that have insurance often claim that it is quite restrictive. The conditions can be quite onerous and even adversely affect your decisions. Here are some of the restrictions often found in marine insurance policies:

Location

Insurance companies often insist that you are in a certain location at a certain time of year, usually out of the cyclone belt. This can add stress to your cruising life and can often be dangerous. Say you are in Fiji in November. To comply with their insurance requirements, many yachtsmen head for New Zealand. However, that journey can be extremely perilous and many boats have been lost in unforecast storms, such as the famous, Queen's Birthday Storm that sunk a number of boats with many sailors needing rescue and two who were not so lucky.

It is arguably, safer for the boat to find a storm mooring in one of the more secure bays in Fiji. It is certainly safer for skipper and crew (who can go ashore if a cyclone is forecast), but the thought of financial loss from not being insured often pushes yachtsmen to make inappropriate decisions – they may decide to head for New Zealand even if it means leaving Fiji in inclement weather and taking on a difficult passage that they, their crew or their boat, may not really be ready for. At the very least, there is a conflict of interests here.

Crew

Many insurance risks are calculated on statistics that do not tell the whole story. For example, many insurance policies insist that a couple take on a third crew member for ocean passages because statistics show that those that do, cope better with problems en route. However, the wrong crew member (and most people fit into this category) can spoil your whole experience and will not be nearly as reliable or efficient as a wind vane self steering (see chapter 13). Also, a wind vane doesn't have demands or get in the way. To be fair, some more enlightened insurance companies are beginning to recognize this, but many still insist upon a third body on board.

Bureaucracy

Many insurance companies will ask you to have your boat surveyed from time to time. Surveys are not cheap. A marine surveyor will not survey the rig or the engine, so you may need to pay out for three surveys if the insurance company requires it.

Show me the money again

In the end, it is all about the money. If a good insurance policy cost a dollar, we would all have one. But they don't.
As a sailor on a budget, you will often be forced to think not whether it is wise to be insured per se, but whether that money might be better spent preventing the type of accident that would require a claim. Surely it is better to have an uninsured yacht with good anchoring gear than an insured one without? Because you have a modest boat without too many electronic toys, a lightning strike will likely only cost you a couple of thousand dollars anyway, making it uneconomical to make a claim. (Most insurance policies have an excess of about $1500, so a claim for $2000 would only net you $500 and cost you your no-claims discount the next time you insure). That is of course, if the insurance company agrees to pay in the first place. Is that really worth all those conditions

and paperwork that impinge on your freedom?

Third Party Only.

This costs around one fifth of the comprehensive premium and protects you from the damage you do to other boats - a bill that in theory could be huge. Many marinas insist you have at least this level of coverage before you enter, but as a good sea gypsy lives at anchor, walloping a mega yacht in the marina is quite a difficult thing to do. However, if for any reason you do hit another boat and the owner sues, you could lose everything you have - so it very much depends on what you have. If you have a nice house that is rented out and bringing in income while you goof off on the big blue, then you may want to splash out a few bucks on third party insurance (particularly while you are new at it!). If the totality of your possessions is a signed picture of Bono, a *My Chemical Romance* t-shirt and some cheese you found behind the cooker, then nobody is actually going to sue you. The boat you hit, will of course, be out of pocket, so it is up to your conscience what to do.

The best insurance is to buy a modest boat that you can replace fairly easily, is unlikely to drag at anchor and won't cause too much damage if it glances off another boat
.

If you are too poor to afford even third party insurance, the least you should do is behave as if you don't have insurance – give every obstacle a wide berth, anchor further away from obstacles than other boats do, be the first to put out a second anchor, reef down earlier, use defensive (rather than competitive) sailing tactics. In other words, develop better seamanship than most other sailors. Prevention is always better than cure and this is doubly so for the uninsured.

For us sea gypsies it all comes down to using our financial resources as best we can – not simply adding something else to our shopping list. Once you have a strong boat and good ground tackle, you can decide about insurance.

Having said all that, some insurance companies are now being run by ex-sailors who know a little of the subject, have identified the relatively low risk group of live-aboard sailors like us who own modest sea boats (i.e. cheap to replace and unlikely to sink) and offer accordingly lower premiums. For the first time, thanks to Topsail Insurance, we have a little insurance ourselves.

So you could say we have a foot in each camp, but take note – we only considered this after the premiums became reasonable and after we had made our floating home as strong and as safe as possible. If you have bought a modest boat and you have limited resources to fit her out, then I certainly do not advise putting insurance at the top of your shopping list ahead of say, good chain and anchors!

As long as we have a little extra cash and companies like Topsail continue to provide cheap, relatively unrestrictive policies for the budget sailor, we will be insured. If the premiums go up again or the company starts demanding we take extra crew or fit bow thrusters, etc, we will go back to self-insuring.

Finally, a quick reminder that insurance premiums increase with the value of the boat. So whether you decide to insure or self insure, you will (again) reap the seemingly endless benefits of having chosen a modest, strong sea boat over an expensive, flashy, bleach bottle full of unnecessary gadgets.

Chapter 21

Staying Together - Relationships on Board

There is only one thing better than cruising around tropical islands without a care in the world on your own private yacht - and that is doing it with someone eminently squeezable.
But be careful! Living on a boat with your partner can place a lot of strain on many relationships. It is often said that people buy a boat in order to split up!

There are certainly elements of truth in this statement and we need to know where these elements are lurking if we are hoping to sail off into a romantic tropical sunset with our main squeeze on board. From what we have observed, there seems to be two principle reasons why relationships fail on a boat.

1. The relationship had already passed its 'sell-by' date.

Nobody can deny that some relationships fail and there is nothing we can do about it. Quite often, we hold on to them long after they are good for either party and some even become quite destructive. If your relationship has deteriorated to this point, it is unlikely to survive the change of life to sea gypsy status. For some, it might be a voyage of re-discovery, but I generally do not observe this to be the case. So if you wish to get your relationship back on track, becoming a sea gypsy is perhaps not the best way to go.

There is a tendency for most of us to equate longevity with

quality (a relationship is 'good' because it lasts and every relationship that lasts is by definition, 'good'). However, notwithstanding the occasional couple who have been in love since high school, the experience of most people is otherwise.

Through the course of their lives, most people find that at least some relationships need to be abandoned. Moving to another country and living in a small space will certainly hasten the process, but is that such a bad thing? In this age of Jerry Springer and Oprah, it almost goes unchallenged that all relationships must be 'saved' with 'work', but fashion and truth have, fortunately, never been the same thing.

If you are in a loving relationship right now, look over at your partner and take a moment to appreciate how lucky you are to have found this person. Good. Now here is an absolute truth: Unless this is the first person you ever kissed, you have had to break off other relationships to get to this point. Are you going to say that ending your previous relationships was a mistake? If you truly believe that, I would keep it quiet from your current squeeze.

The point is that some things must pass in order for new things to grow, and this is not the ultimate disaster that it is portrayed to be on Oprah. If you hadn't been part of that process, you would not have found the wonderful partner you have now. Becoming a sea gypsy may hasten this process, but that is fine and natural. Breathe deeply. Let it work.

2. Too much, too soon.

Pushing your partner too hard is the quickest way to lose

them. If I had a dollar for every time I have seen a couple shouting at each other while docking or performing some other routine sailing task, I could afford to pay Jimmy Buffet to stop singing.

Writing here in Nuku Hiva, I was discussing this thought with an old salt who had worked the fisheries back in the 80s in Shark Bay, Western Australia. Shark bay is 30 miles or so across and 60 miles long. It is completely open to the west and can develop a huge swell quite quickly when the wind is from that quarter. Every weekend, he would pull some crying person (usually female) from the deck of a boat while some silent, taciturn person (usually male) took the boat back to harbour. He would chuck a blanket around the shoulders of the weeping person and head to the shore with the constant refrain of "never again" ringing in his ears.

This is a far more serious problem in many ways because it can wreck otherwise good relationships and nobody wants that. Here is what usually happens (I apologize for the gender split, but it is nearly always like this):

- Couple agrees to do something on a sailboat and crossing oceans or sailing around the world seems like the thing to do.

- They set off voyaging too soon (often on the wrong boat).

- Stress (caused by fear and money worries) and poor communication leads to shouting and fighting and general breakdown of the relationship.

As it is so important to break this all too common chain of events, let us examine some of them in more detail.

Couple agrees to do something on a sailboat and crossing oceans or sailing around the world seems like the thing to do.

Fortunately, the sea gypsy approach nips much of this in the bud. Firstly and most importantly (at the risk of being repetitive) do not set out to buy a boat and sail around the world. This is the decision that all further problems will inevitably be traced back to as you fight the clock to prepare yourselves and the boat.

'Too much, too soon' will end your sailing relationship quicker than a hole in the bilge. The decision to sail around the world must come once you have decided you actually like living together on a boat, in much the same way as you don't ask someone to marry you five minutes after meeting them. You must be sure you are compatible before you pop the question - and not just in the first throes of lust.

As stated exhaustively in chapter 2, pick a nice place to buy and refit your boat and learn by gradually pushing your comfort zone. You and your partner will become closer as you learn your sea-craft and build your confidence together. Sure you will make mistakes, but together.

Work like this and you will be laughing about, and learning from your mistakes over a coconut cocktail sprinkled with unimaginable amounts of giggles, rather than fighting your way through the foggy marshes of recrimination and blame. Not only will your triumphs make you both deservedly proud, they also create a shared history and reinforce bonds.

Doesn't this sound better than the sweating, unconfident 'skipper' yelling at the crying, terrified 'crew'?

Furthermore, if you are hoping to persuade an equally inexperienced partner to come with you, what do you think will work best:

a. Let's sail around the world! Through all the great Capes and the roaring 40s! (gulp!)

b. Do you fancy drifting around the Caribbean for a romantic year or two and learning how to live on the sea?

The beauty of the sea gypsy approach is that if you do end up doing (a), you will have needed to do (b) anyway to get the experience. You might be lucky and get away with (a) without doing (b), but the confidence you will gain will turn the experience from one nail biting fear-fest after another, into a truly rewarding journey (as well as increase your chances of surviving it).

They set off voyaging too soon (often on the wrong boat).

Take your time! Find the right boat. Leave your goal-orientated mind on land where it belongs and concentrate on making this an enjoyable experience for all involved. Learn your craft and build your knowledge in an enjoyable, loving and mutually supportive way. Explore your wonderful new gypsy life, read the books you always wanted to. Sail in the local regatta and take multi-day trips to local beauty spots for romantic dinners and goodly amounts of gratuitous bonking. Before you know it, living and travelling on the briny water will assimilate in your minds and seem perfectly natural.

You will know when your partner is ready for a bigger challenge by the way she looks out across the horizon, by her confidence in bad weather and by her obvious feelings of accomplishment (rather than fear) when things get rough. You cannot rush this and it cannot be bought, so don't even try - if this is the partner you want to keep.

Smiles on deck, not miles under the keel! This is the mantra of the happy sailing couple.

Stress and poor communication leads to shouting

This is another all-too-common dynamic that needs to be nipped in the bud.

For men (again I apologize for the gender split, but it is real enough) much of this comes from performance anxiety. In other words, men seem quite nervous about 'getting it wrong' and looking dumb. You can't be 'caught out' or look dumb if you have already admitted you don't have clue, so don't set yourself up for stress by claiming to be a good sailor and then start competing with all the other egos. Start you new life as a self-confessed novice and sailing idiot and then try and live up to it.

Women on the other hand seem to be more stressed by lack

of information. In a meeting of women sailors that Jasna attended in 2013, the main complaint amongst the attendees was that they would like to know more about sailing, but their partner did not have the patience to teach them.

I cannot understand the mentality of men who are playing this power game by keeping all the information to themselves (any more than I can understand women who agree to buy a boat without taking any interest in the physics of sailing). I suspect in many cases that this is because the men have not taken the time to learn themselves and therefore cannot explain to their spouses for the simple reason that they do not know the answers.

Not knowing the answer is not a problem unless you have set yourself up as the 'all knowing skipper.' If you have decided to learn together, then you can find the answers together. Then, when your spouse asks you a question, that is what you hear, a question - not an ego-bruising accusation of incompetence. When your partner asks you why it is important to have the correct camber on your mainsail, you just say 'damned if I know' and go look it up together. Find the answer and then go and put it into practice together. Remember, you are trying to build an effective team here!

Every relationship is different, but patience and understanding are important to all of them - and the more stressed you are, the less likely it is that these qualities will float to the surface and find corporeal form. The more you allow 'goal-seeking' or 'performance expectations' to creep into your behaviour or set your agenda, the more stressed you are going to be and the less satisfying your relationship will become.

Finally, it is wise to remember what our good friend and adventurous Cape Horn sailor Peter Cookingham says:

Teach your spouse everything you know and be nicer to her than you were on land because not only should she be able to pick you up if you fall overboard, she will have to want to as well!

Afterword – Staying Sane.

We hope that this book has achieved its purpose by demonstrating that, with a little shift in attitude, great adventures can be had without great amounts of cash.

Attitude, that's the thing!

Enjoyment of the sea gypsy life is dependent on it and most problems can be traced back to the wrong version of it. If there is anything that is vague or unclear, feel free to drop us a line. Before we go though, we would like to remind all potential sea gypsies that although you will pour your energy and soul into your boat, it is important to remember this one vital truth:

It's just a boat.

Do not defend it with your life or your health.

Below are some true stories.

Racing sailor, master sail maker and all-round jolly good bloke, Mike Danielson was racing aboard the yacht *Blue* in the Banderas Bay Regatta. As the yachts jostled for position at the start line it appeared that *Blue*'s transom would touch another yacht. Mike sprang aft to fend the other yacht off and both his legs were shattered between the two hulls.

When hurricane Odile approached La Paz in Mexico, two very good friends of ours decided to stay onboard their boat at anchor, despite the ominous forecast. They had virtually rebuilt their cement ketch from the hull upwards and had far too much sweat invested in her to leave her to fend for herself. So they stayed onboard to defend her. The bodies of these two wonderful sea gypsies were later found washed up in the mangroves.

An American couple in the Caribbean returned to their boat after a drink ashore to find a dinghy already attached to it and people moving around below by torchlight. They decided to confront the intruders. I will not disturb you by detailing the outcome of this misadventure, but only the wife lived to tell the tale, and only just.

The legendary sailor Sir Peter Blake (one of the few sailors to ever rack up half a million ocean miles) was shot and killed when he produced a gun to resist thieves attempting to board his vessel in the Amazon Basin. The thieves took what they wanted and left the rest of the crew unharmed.

All of the above tragedies (and dozens more like them) can be avoided if you always remember… it's only a boat! I love my boat too, but she is not worth risking my life, my health, or the life and health of my partner.

If there is a hurricane approaching your anchorage and there is not time to sail away, put out all the anchors you can, batten down the hatches, go ashore and huddle in the church or wherever the locals hide. If there are a couple of intruders on your boat, let them take what they want – after all, a sea gypsy doesn't have much worth stealing anyway. Do not defend your possessions with your life. Certainly never use your valuable body as a human fender.

Get real! –this is not the movies and you are not Bruce Willis. Not even Bruce Willis is really Bruce Willis and you need your body in good shape in order to move your mouth to restaurants.

Accidents and fatalities are rare on boats and once you remove all the tragedies that are avoidable with the right attitude, they are virtually non-existent. If you can divest yourself of the competitive impulse, of goal-setting behaviour and always remember that, in the end 'it's just a boat', you will have a long and happy sea gypsy life on our wonderful blue planet.

Fair winds and good luck to you!

Rick Page and Jasna Tuta
19°29.30'S
178°56.40'E
August 2015

.

About the Authors

Rick Page holds an honours degree in Disaster Engineering and Management and is a contributor to *Cruising Helmsman* and *Cruising World* magazines. He became a RYA qualified skipper in 2008 and has lived aboard every day since 2007 when he bought his first boat *Marutji* – a steel Van de Stadt 34 (pictured on the cover).

Jasna Tuta is a former primary school teacher. She has been living the sea gypsy life since 2010 and has published over 200 magazine pages and 64 radio shows. *Marutji* was also her first boat. She regularly holds sailing courses and talks in Italy and Slovenia, splices rope to chain like it was spaghetti, makes the world's best lasagna and is genetically half-fish (the good half).

They are both living aboard their current boat *Calypso* somewhere in the Pacific.

Connect with us:

Blog: **www.sailingcalypso.com/**

Email: **sailingcalypso@gmail.com**

Facebook page: **Sailing Calypso**

***

Acknowledgements

Many thanks to Topsail Insurance in the UK for making insurance a reality for poor sea gypsies.

We would also like to thank Advanced Elements of California for negotiating Polynesian Customs and Excise (at great expense to themselves) to get our new kayak to us in Tahiti.

Ben Fogle and the *New Lives in the Wild* team deserve a special mention for helping us spread the sea gypsy ethos to an entirely new audience (thanks to Bravo the sound guy for our new 'washing machine') and Ed Page, for putting the whole thing together.

Finally, we would like to thank His Holiness King Neptune for his continuing support on the big blue and for providing us with all the fish.

***

Thank you for reading our book.

If you enjoyed it, please take a moment to leave us a review at your favourite retailer because we could use the sails (this is not a spelling error, this is what we actually buy with the money).

If you did not enjoy it, we are sorry, but we would still like to take this opportunity to thank you for the cash and for hearing us out.

Recommended Reading

The Boat Owner's Mechanical and Electrical Manual by Nigel Calder

The Complete Ocean Skipper by Tom Cunliffe

20 Small Sailboats That Will Take You Around the World by John Vigor

The Cost Conscious Cruiser by Lin and Larry Pardey

Sailing the Farm by Ken Neumeyer

Seaworthiness: The Forgotten Factor by C A Marchaj

Voyaging on a Small Income by Annie Hill

Storm Tactics by Lin and Larry Pardey

Zen and the Art of Motorcycle Maintenance by Robert M Pirsig

Recommended Gear

For details and reviews of all the gear we recommend in this book, see our website www.sailingcalypso.com